SAILING UPHILL

A winter outing on the lower Columbia River aboard Gander II.

SAILING UPHILL

An Unconventional Life on the Water

Sam McKinney

Horsdal & Schubart

Horsdal & Schubart Publishers Ltd.
Victoria, BC, Canada

Front-cover photograph: *Northern Spray*, courtesy of Captain John Porter. Back-cover photograph and photographs in the text: courtesy of the author.

Section and chapter-head drawings by Pat McCallum, Victoria, BC.

This book is set in Aldine 401 Book Text.

Horsdal & Schubart wishes to acknowledge the Canada Council for the Arts, Heritage Canada through the Book Industry Development Program and the British Columbia Arts Council for their financial support of our publishing program.

Printed and bound in Canada by Printcrafters, Winnipeg, Manitoba.

Canadian Cataloguing in Publication Data

McKinney, Sam, 1927-
  Sailing uphill

ISBN 0-920663-70-2

  1. McKinney, Sam, 1927- 2. Boatmen—Canada—Biography. 3. Boats and boating—Canada. 4. Boats and boating—United States. I. Title.

GV776.15.A2M35 2000   797.1'092   C00-910801-7

Printed and bound in Canada

For Gail, who never asked "Why?"

"So we beat on, boats against the current, borne back
ceaselessly into the past."
F. Scott Fitzgerald

CONTENTS

Acknowledgments   ix

SECTION ONE:
BOATS AND SHIPS, A RIVER AND THE SEA

Chapter One – A Boy and a Rowboat   2
Chapter Two – Village of My Twelfth Summer   8
Chapter Three – Deckboy on the Last Sternwheeler   12
Chapter Four – Away to Sea   16
Chapter Five – My Last Ship   21
Chapter Six – Almost to Tahiti   28
Chapter Seven – Shipwrecked in Mexico   32
Chapter Eight – Northwest Waters   38
Chapter Nine – Islands   47
Chapter Ten – A Schooner Called *Heritage*   57

SECTION TWO
VOYAGE ACROSS NORTH AMERICA

Chapter One – *Gander* Up the Columbia River   62
Chapter Two – *Gander* Up the Snake River   72
Chapter Three – Shipwrecked in Montana   77
Chapter Four – Down the Missouri River   85
Chapter Five – Lakes of the River   90
Chapter Six – Counting Backwards, Mile 734 to 0   106
Chapter Seven – To Chicago and Georgian Bay   110
Chapter Eight – The Trent-Severn Waterway and the
    St. Lawrence River   123
Chapter Nine – Down to the Atlantic   132

SECTION THREE
WOODEN BOATS, WESTERN WATERS

Chapter One – *Reach of Tide*   142
Chapter Two – Rowing to Astoria   145
Chapter Three – A Yawl Called *Spray*   151
Chapter Four – Requiem for My Heroes   158

Postscript   162

ACKNOWLEDGMENTS

THE BOOKS AND WRITINGS of other men who sometimes inspired me, or expressed better than I could certain thoughts, emotions and philosophies, are quoted throughout my memoirs. The thoughts I borrowed should be given the proper citations of book title, publisher and page number, but I have a lifetime's collection of such thoughts, some of them as scraps of paper tossed into a folder, others scribbled on the edges of charts, still others in the log books of my various voyages. All are filed in this haphazard method without their appropriate source references. Therefore, my apologies to the following.

To my writer-friend Don Berry for borrowing his wonderful words about the pleasure of building a boat in *To Build a Ship*. Not only did I borrow his comment to explain how I felt as a boy building a boat, but I also hung it on the wall of the boatshop where I built some of my boats. You got it just right, Don.

I would like to have read the French writer Henri Troya's memoirs, set down when he was 80, but I just borrowed the quote from a newspaper review of his book.

My "Island Notes" are a large part of my borrowed quotes. My favorite is the one by anthropologist Loren Eiseley, and writer Lawrence Durrell is also in that collection.

James Ronda is a distinguished Western historian and a Lewis and Clark scholar. I thought his description of what it meant to native Americans to have their place names replaced by white explorers appropriate, and included it as something of an apology to those people. Writer Barry Lopez is quoted because I think he gave a good rationale as to why explorers left new place names in their wakes.

The wonderful passage of the old sailor rat from Kenneth Grahame's *The Wind in the Willows* I can cite, because I have the book: page 173, Scribner's, New York, 1953.

Long out of print is Stewart Holbrook's book on the Columbia River, from which I borrowed his accurate description of Wallula Gap.

I would like to know the "unknown" Arabian poet I quote. His line "The people are more generous than nature" fits not only the kindness of the Montana people who helped me out of that particular predicament, but the many others who so often saved me from other problems of storm, wind and running out of gas.

My copy of A.B. Guthrie's *The Big Sky* went down with the *Gander II* in that Montana shipwreck, but his character saw that mighty river just right.

John Neihardt's book recounting his canoe voyage down the Missouri (I think it was titled *The River and I*) was also lost in that shipwreck. I liked it; it was somewhat parallel to my own story, both describing men whipped and damn near beaten by Old Muddy.

A copy of Joshua Slocum's *Sailing Alone Around the World* came with my purchase of the *Northern Spray*. The line "As for a ship to command ..." apears on page 4 of the 1956 edition, Dover Publications, New York.

Another book that came with the boat was R. Bruce Roberts-Goodson's *Spray, The Ultimate Cruising Boat*. From this, I borrowed some of marine architect C. Andrade, Jr.'s, article that first appeared in a June 1909 issue of *Rudder* magazine.

The oldest clipped quote in my collection dates back to the days of my early manhood. What more does a young fellow thinking about going to sea need than the advice of Harry Pidgeon: "You can sail for one day, can't you? That's all it is — one day after another."

And so, this note on my sources. More than just quotes, they include some of the philosophies I have tried to live by. I thank all of you for your handed-down wisdom, and pass along your thoughts for others to contemplate.

Sam McKinney, June 2000

SECTION ONE

BOATS AND SHIPS, A RIVER AND THE SEA

CHAPTER ONE

A BOY AND A ROWBOAT

I N KANSAS CITY, MISSOURI, by the muddy waters of the
Missouri River, so my mother tells me, I built my first boat out
of a shoebox. I was then five years old. That first boat I do not
remember but whatever impulse it was that made me fashion a
boat out of a shoebox in that far-from-the-sea inland city has
stayed with me for more than a half century as passion, profession
and enduring pursuit of all things connected with boats and ships,
rivers and the sea.

My father died when I was six and my mother and I — she
widowed and nearly penniless in the 1930s Depression years —
moved from Kansas City to Portland, Oregon, to live with her
sister and brother-in-law, my aunt and uncle.

That uncle took charge of me, a fatherless kid, and gave me
everything and more that a boy could ever ask of a surrogate father,
including instructions on fishing, camping and, most importantly,
boating. He was a bear of a man, his looks a combination — as I

2

remember him — of Teddy Roosevelt and Clark Gable, and his laugh was like the bellow of a bull sea lion.

He had a workshop at the back of his garage and one day, he backed his car into the driveway and unloaded a roof-top load of lumber. He piled the planks along one side of the garage, placed two sawhorses in the middle of the garage and said very simply, "We're going to build a boat."

Oh, what a man can do with a few tools, some boards, and a boy to help: everything worth doing, the essentials of an education — how to scribe and saw a beveled line, hammer in a nail, plane the edge of a board, drill a hole, paint, caulk and tie a knot. Patient was my uncle as teacher, attentive and eager was I as his apprentice. He would demonstrate how to do a task, I would try to copy what he did. I made mistakes, suffered numerous cuts and scrapes. But magic was taking place in that garage, board by board, plank by plank, to produce that wonderful thing called a boat.

To build a boat, I believe, is a special kind of experience, an experience apart from the building of any other form or structure. The demands imposed by the critical measurements of line and shape impose a stern discipline which makes the building process a challenge.

My uncle and I, without too many words, just built a rowboat. But subconsciously, we were experiencing the pleasure and the excitement that writer Don Berry describes in his book *To Build a Ship*.

At first it was like the beginning of a love affair. We tended to go around grinning foolishly at each other ... because we shared a secret that nobody else could touch. We were going to build a Ship. ... For the first time I understood things about the Revolution, things the history books left out. One fact that never gets written down is the feeling a man suddenly gets in his belly that he can change the way things are. With the strength of his back and arms and brain, he can make things different, and he doesn't have to put up with it any more, whatever 'it' may be. ... There is no other feeling like that known to humankind. ... For the first time he realizes there is more to living than merely submitting.

The building of that rowboat, I think, was the seminal experience of my life. More than acquiring a beginning knowledge in the use of a saw, plane and chisel, the building of that boat showed me what a person could accomplish by the simple process of just trying, of finding in the unknown the beginning point of knowing.

My uncle moored the boat on the Columbia River and on Saturdays during the summer, I would ride my bike to the river and take the boat out on short fishing trips. On one of those trips, I was too intent on fishing to notice the rising wind that came with the rain. When I became aware of it, it was too late. I sat helplessly while the wind took charge of the boat, blowing it farther offshore. For a moment I panicked as the waves crested in small whitecaps that slopped water over the bow of the boat. I rowed with all my strength, but I could make no headway against the wind and I sat transfixed by fear, looking only at the safe shore I could not reach. Then turning, I saw ahead in the path of the wind the surf-fringed outline of a small island. Now desperately, I started rowing again, rowing hard toward the island, afraid the wind would carry me past it. Tears mixed with rain ran down my face, my mouth wide open to suck in gasping breaths of air as the little oars wind-milled through wind and water.

We hit the shore with a bump that sent me sprawling in the bottom of the boat. For a few seconds I lay there, breathless, looking up, a canopied ceiling of wind-torn black and gray clouds sweeping overhead, the rain falling wet and cold on my face.

The boat had landed on a gravel beach that shelved upwards to a line of low brush and trees. I stood up and stepped out of the boat onto the beach and looked out across the black waves running under the darkening evening sky.

Looking for another boat, for someone, for something. But there was nothing. I was alone, frightened, wet and hungry. Worst of all was the gathering darkness, the beginning of night. Again, I stared outward from the island, not wanting to accept my fate: that I would have to spend the night on the island.

Instincts set my body and mind in motion. I pulled the boat up the beach, unloaded the fishing pole, tackle box and my three small fish. I lifted the boat, turned it over, and propped up one side with the two oars. It made a small shelter, rock-floored but out of the wind and rain. I crawled beneath the boat and sat there shivering. To survive the wet, cold night, I knew I had to have the warmth of a fire. But how could I build a fire? Then I remembered that in the tackle box I had six matches stuck together in a paraffin wrapper.

From the high-water line of the beach, I gathered sticks and small branches, some of them almost dry. Just outside the edge of the tipped-up boat I made a ring of small rocks and in the circle carefully piled small twigs. With my fishing knife, I carved small shavings from the driest sticks and laid them at the base of the small wood cone.

Just six matches in their paraffin wrapper; I was almost afraid to touch them with wet fingers. I dried my hands on my sweater and then willed them to stop shaking as I lifted out the packet. Two matches were wasted because I struck them on rocks that were too smooth and damp. The third one the wind blew out.

Three matches were left and I picked up one of them, crying, pleading, "Please, please light." It did and I carried it in my cupped hands to the little pile of shavings. There was the flicker of a flame, a thread of smoke, and then nothing. I crawled back under the cover of the boat and huddled there, wet, cold and sobbing.

The paraffin wrapper dangled in my hand, the last two matches sticking to one end. It was not a thought; it was my response to desperation. I lit the fifth match, held it to the wrapper and it ignited. I pushed the flaming wrapper into the cone of shavings, ignoring the searing pain of burnt fingers. The wax bubbled as a tiny inferno ignited the shavings, then the twigs and then the branches, and a smile of joy and surprise creased my wet face.

They were half raw, the three fish I cooked on a stick thrust through their bodies from mouth to tail. I ate them all, bones, guts and fins. In the last light of day, I gathered larger pieces of wood from the beach and piled them like a barricade along the sheltered side of the boat. One by one, as darkness covered the island, I placed them on the fire and then sat with huddled arms staring into the source of heat and light I had created. Stared and slept with my head on my knees. Woke, fed the fire, and at last lay down in the shelter of the boat and slept.

Sunlight, seeping in under the boat, awakened me to a calm and lovely morning. Quickly, I launched the boat and rowed back to the dock, knowing that my night of adventure would now have its price. They met me at the dock, my mother, my newly acquired stepfather and my uncle.

My return to my family was first met with tears of joy and relief. I could not answer all the rapid-fire questions.

"What were you doing out there?"

"Why did you go out there?"

"The wind, it carried me out," was the only defense I could offer.

It was not enough. Joy at my safe return became edged with anger.

From my poor mother: "Do you realize you could have drowned?"

From my stepfather: "Do you realize how worried you mother was?"

From my mother: "Promise me you'll never go out in that boat again."

From my uncle: "Guess we'll have to get you a bigger boat."

Oh Uncle, you understood, didn't you? That that night alone on the island in the storm, the little fire I built, the protecting shelter of the upturned boat — those things were my rite of passage, my introduction to fear, to danger, to aloneness, to self dependence. You understood what no one else did, that something of me had stayed behind on the island: some part of me I would go looking for that would be found waiting at the end of other voyages to other islands.

I dedicated my first book to that uncle, a book about the Columbia River where I made that first voyage. It read: "To my uncle Ivan. When I was a boy, he gave me a boat and oars, and sent me on my way."

My stepfather also played a part in my youthful pursuit of boating adventures because he represented everything I wanted to avoid. When he mowed the lawn, he wore a gray hat and rubbers over his wing-tipped shoes. There would be no sunburned brow or wet feet for this man, not ever. The world to him, and life itself, was charted with the list of things that had to be done, and there was no way to avoid these dreary, treadmill tasks. He was kind and gentle and honestly concerned about my welfare, and he saw it as his duty to save me from myself and peril by extolling the virtues of thrift, moderation and security.

One incident that I remember illustrated the difference in outlook between this practical man and my romantic, optimistic self as a boy. From somewhere I had salvaged the broken rudder and tiller of an old sailboat. It was my most valuable possession, the beginning for a second boat. With a rudder and a tiller, as I saw the world, all that was needed for the complete boat was a little luck and time. As my stepfather saw the world, the tiller was good for an axe handle, the rudder for firewood, and there went my plan to build a second boat.

Not cruel at all this man, he was just making practical use of something he thought useless. And as in most things he did, there was a lesson for me to learn: that you can't reach for the stars at the neglect of bread and butter, shirts and shoes. Many times in my life, I have wondered how I would have turned out had I followed the wise guidance of this man, taken over his small, one-man paint business after his death and settled in to pursue his modest goals of comfort and security.

Ah yes; bills paid, feet dry; no need to sit huddled in an open boat on the dark side of dawn, to eat cold beans out of a can, sleep in last week's dirty clothes, worry about the wind, watch the gathering waves, sacrifice love, contentment, success and security. And no voice of a nameless poet taunting me:

Onward into dangers
Where a thousand years ago
I was in my dreams.

CHAPTER TWO

VILLAGE OF MY TWELFTH SUMMER

THE CROWNING ADVENTURE OF my youth occurred in my twelfth summer when a school friend invited me to spend a summer with his grandmother who lived in an old fishing village on the lower Columbia River.

Our four parents assembled to discuss this invitation. They could see only danger in such a place. Questions: How close to the village is the river? Will they actually be on a boat? Will they be warm and dry? The answer to each question increased their apprehension.

I wanted to scream: "What difference does it make? Can't you say yes to something different just once in your life and then see what will happen?"

It was probably the white-haired grandmother who carried the day.

"Nothing to worry about," she reassured them. "They will have a warm bedroom and the river in front of the village is a shallow tidal flat. Very safe."

On her word to watch out for us, permission was granted and away we went, my cardboard box packed with warm clothes, a toothbrush, comb, bar of soap and my mother's list of rules for table manners, bedtime and bathing. Once in the village, however, the grandmother dropped her motherly way and laid down her rules, simple and to the point.

"Houses," she said, "were not made for boys. You will sleep in the barn, stay out of the parlor, come into the kitchen only for meals, and keep the wood box filled." So my friend — Bob was his name — and I slept in the hay loft in the barn, our blankets two deer skins, not too well cured. We shared the loft with bats overhead, mice in the straw, and the cows and chickens below.

Vividly, I remember the dawn awakenings in that loft: the soft, clucking noises of the chickens, the discordant crowing of roosters and the sound of cows stamping their feet in their stalls. The sun, coming through cracks in the walls, made shafts of light and turned the hay dust of our straw beds to gold when we got up. These domestic arrangements suited us perfectly. So did the food. For breakfast, eggs and homemade bread. For lunch, fried sturgeon, boiled potatoes and fresh milk with the leftovers served for dinner. The potatoes we grew, the milk came from our cow. The sturgeon, too small to be sold commercially, were tied tail-first to the bank of a small creek and pulled in when needed.

As boys, we were not idle long in a working fishing village. "You will go with Fred in the boat," the elders had decided. Fred had been born in Finland and behind him when he emigrated to the Columbia River were generations of fishermen. Thousands of other Scandinavians had settled in small villages along the lower Columbia, still maintaining the language, culture and traditional way of their North Sea lives. What English Fred knew was largely limited to swear words, but to Bob and me, he was a kind of god because of his understanding of boats and the art of fishing.

We went out fishing almost every night. Bob and I would try to guess ahead the place where Fred would drop the gillnet, already testing our knowledge against the day when such a decision might be ours to make.

Fred's boat was a traditional wooden, double-ended Columbia River fishboat. The engine was housed aft under a tiny cabin. The net was piled in the fore-part of the boat where it could be paid out through a roller on one side of the boat in what was called a "drift."

For Bob and me, the boat was our nighttime, no-nonsense classroom and its rules were the harsh and inflexible laws of the river's currents, winds and waves. The punishment for failure was a sound cussing by Fred in both English and Finnish, a lost fish, and sometimes a push overboard for a swim in a cold river. It was hard, cold work out on the river at night. The net was heavy, the sharp fins of the salmon cut our hands, and the open boat gave us no shelter from frequent night fog and rain. Bob and I might have cried in the night but we never complained. We were a working part of the river, the boat, and the proud tradition of fishing.

With the net out, we would drift and Fred would instruct us in another phase of our growing-up education, sex and swearing. Sex education was by song, the lusty, bawdy ballads sung by Fred. They lacked romance and biology but we were left with no doubts about the ways of nature. The whole process — as described in Fred's songs — struck us as being vastly hilarious. And we learned to swear with bilingual proficiency.

So the hours of the first drift would pass with the sun dropping over the distant line of the river bar. Sometimes a moon would rise, sometimes we were surrounded by an utterly black night with only the tiny light at the end of the curved net twinkling in the dark water. Fred would haul in the net by hand while Bob and I pulled at the long sweep to keep the boat perpendicular to the net. Then, with Fred pulling and swearing and the two of us on the sweep, the magic would begin as the gleaming salmon were pulled from the dark river. Great wet things they were, to be tossed at our feet where we stood holding onto the oar in the empty net deck. Up to our ankles and then our knees they would pile as we slid and slithered in blood and slime, still keeping to the pull of the sweep.

After midnight, we would lay out a second drift. Then we would sleep curled up in the bottom of the boat, no bed, no blanket, but sleep never deeper with Fred humming some verse over us as he kept watch. In the morning with a load of fish, we would head across the Columbia for Astoria and the cannery docks. While Bob and I unloaded the fish, Fred would go up town for an hour or so, and return to the boat drunk. Fred's working day was over when he returned and it was our job to take the boat home while he slept.

Our village lay some 12 miles across and up the Columbia. Our course had to clear sandbars, the seine nets, and the ferry lane, and then thread the shallows of Grays Bay. We had never been given instructions on how to take the boat home, but one morning, after we had made the trip numerous times, Fred gave us the wheel and the short order: "Take us home." From then on, the homeward-bound voyage was our command.

Back in the village, our work was over and the day — with infinite possibilities — was ours. We ran naked most of the time, the villagers being old and no girls about to shame our Adam-like innocence. Besides, our clothes, after many nights in the fishboat, grew a little strong in the sun. It never occurred to us to wash them. Like natives, we gathered wild berries from bushes, picked apples from the trees, and dug with our hands for licorice roots in the soft moss of the woods. The villagers left us alone. We were expected to be nothing more than boys: half-savage, dirty, self-sufficient and always hungry.

From the village dock, we acquired two unused wooden fish boxes. These we patched, and with the remains of an old tarp, we made sails. I shudder today when I recall the voyages we made along the shores of the lower Columbia in those two frail, makeshift boats made out of boxes only four feet long.

There was only one blot in my village summer by the river. My mother had given me a new toothbrush with a note to remind me to brush my teeth every day. Stuck in a crack in the barn wall and never used, that toothbrush became the symbol of the world that lay outside the village of docks and fishboats, a world to which I never wanted to return. What I wanted was that oldest boyhood dream: to run away to sea.

CHAPTER THREE

DECKBOY ON THE LAST STERNWHEELER

MY FIRST STEP IN the direction of "running away to sea" was taken the day I went job hunting along the Portland waterfront. I was just 16 and it took all my courage to present myself at the front office of one of the city's river transportation companies. To my astonishment, I was hired and given the job as deckboy on one of the last old sternwheelers working the river. I got the job, not because of my fishboat experience, but because a husky boy of 16 could get a job anywhere during the manpower shortage of World War II.

As deckboy, I was at the bottom of the hierarchy on the sternwheeler. Anyone could order me about, even the cook. My working hours were whenever I was needed, which was most of the time, day or night. I wasn't called by my name, just "Boy" followed by an order to do this or do that or a "Get the hell out of the way."

The rivermen who worked the Columbia were a rough, tough and tradition-proud bunch. It was Fred and the fishboat all over again, only on the sternwheeler the dangers were far greater, the work harder and the cussing-outs continuous. To be accepted — to survive — a deckboy had to endure without complaint an agony of hard work, verbal abuse and sometimes a kick in the pants. I endured — and survived — all three.

The sternwheeler towed log rafts from the lower Columbia to an upriver paper mill. The logs first had to be bundled together with steel cables to form rafts. My job was to work the huge steam winch on the foredeck of the boat that pulled the cables tight around the rafts. Tremendous strains were placed on those cables by the winch under my control and if one of them broke or came loose, it could whip through the air with enough force to kill a man (and a deckboy too, I thought).

I was afraid of the grinding open gears of the spinning drum-heads on the huge winches and the snapping, whipping cables. But that was only fear. What terrorized me was the captain in the pilot house high above me who cursed and damned my every effort to follow his orders.

"Haul in, let out, take up slack … no, no, no, not that way. I said to tighten up, not slack off. Jesus Christ, can't you do anything right? Quit playing with yourself and haul in that cable … or do I have to come down there and do it myself?"

And so it would go, hour after hour, day after day. From where he stood high up in the pilot house he could see everything I did, except for my crying and the tears rolling down my grease-marked cheeks. I cried not because of the work or the cussing but because I wanted to do it right for him, captain-master of the boat.

One day I did something right. As I was letting out the long tow line that pulled the log raft, the winch jammed and instantly the cable tightened to the breaking point. The dog (a metal wedge locking the winch drum) had accidentally dropped in between the teeth of the gears and stopped the turning drum. I grabbed a sledge hammer and knocked it out and the tow line began to unwind. I had saved the cable and probably the winch.

That evening, after all my duties were completed, the captain called for me to come up to the pilot house. He stood before the big spoked wheel, his eyes on the river ahead. Without turning, he spoke to me.

"See that sandbar out there?"
I looked out the pilot house and saw nothing.
"Where?"
"Right off that point. Where the water looks different."
And then, later, "See that snag sticking up? That's where you have to make your turn to get your tow around the bend. Remember that."
Why would I want to remember the location of an old stump? Then it came to me. He was telling me what I would have to know about the river if someday I wanted to stand behind the wheel of a riverboat, a captain myself. Every evening from then on, my lessons in steamboating continued up in the pilot house, he pointing out sandbars, mud banks, hidden pilings, and the deep water of the channel. By day, however, I was still that god-damned kid who didn't know his penis from a peavey, though his curses were sometimes followed by a smile. Once he even called me by name: "Deckboy."

Today, I wonder about boys, wonder about what they do, what they dream about. It seems to me that their adventures — if they can be called that — take place in the institutionalized, commercialized and safe environment of the planned school event, the organized summer camp, the shopping-center mall, the video parlor, the never-never land of TV. Their lives seem to be managed by the professionals, ticket takers, teachers, coaches and corporate advertisers who think of them not as boys but as consumers for logo T-shirts and brand-name running shoes. They have never built a raft, cut a willow for a fish pole, or made soup in a tin can over a bonfire.

That wonderful natural anarchy of the Columbia River shores that was the play land of my youth disappeared long ago. "Danger, Keep Out" signs are posted everywhere worth exploring. Swamps have been drained and chain-link fences, industrial tracts and houseboat marinas ring the river shores. The island where I spent the night beneath that rowboat has been dredged away. None of the little fishing villages of the lower Columbia exist, the salmon are nearly extinct and the old wooden gillnet boats like Fred's are now museum pieces. The last steamboat was retired from the river decades ago. Gone, so much of all of that, villages, docks, fishboats, fish and river steamers, much of it without trace. Gone the men who shared with me their lives, their work and their boats. I am the inheritor of something that no longer exists — the time of my river youth.

What I discovered in that time of youth and adolescence, what that river world presented to me, was a geography of possibilities. There, I learned what was possible in the mixture of sun and river and wind and self. I knew what it was like to stare over the side of a boat into dark water at midnight and see death there in the hissing waves. I knew the dawn of long, cold nights and the return of the sun streaking through fog and I was never the same again. All of this was tied to boats, to the natural world of the river, and to the traditions of the men who worked on the river. For me, it was a milieu of wholeness and integrity that stood for authentic life, an idealized life to strive for.

Impossible and romanticized, of course, were those early ideals that formed my outlook on life. Sensible men are able to laugh at the illusions of untested youth, leave them behind as they go about the practical business of life. I have not been able to do so and I agree with the French writer Henri Troya who, looking back on his life from age 80, wrote that,

> The older you get, the more you realize that you acquired everything from a very early age, that minor events — or events which seemed minor at the time — left a lasting mark on you, and that in the final account the most essential part of your makeup is the child you once were. You may be wrinkled and white-haired, but it's the child in you that lives on, and will probably do so until you breathe your last.

CHAPTER FOUR

AWAY TO SEA

PORTLAND, DURING WORLD WAR II, emerged from its quiet river slumber and became a major ship-building center for Liberty-type cargo carriers and tankers.

Over 300 of these ships were mass-produced in the Portland yards and put in service transporting war supplies and food to the Pacific and Atlantic fronts. To man these ships, the United States Maritime Service opened a recruiting office in the city. At 17 years of age, I joined the service and was sent to the Maritime Training School on Catalina Island off the coast of southern California.

The first few weeks of the training school were modeled along the lines of a navy bootcamp, all marching, drill and physical fitness. Then came four weeks of training in the rudiments of seamanship aboard a school ship, one of them being an old retired Alaskan whaler. At the end of that period, most of the students left the school and were assigned to ships as ordinary seamen.

I qualified to stay on for the advanced training school. Graduation from it permitted a student to sail as an acting able-bodied seaman, an "AB" as he would be called. I loved the school and I was a star student in the classes that taught simple navigation, ship steering, cargo handling, rope work, small-boat handling and sea rescue.

The old "bosuns" who were our instructors frequently salted their lessons with curses and cuffs. I thought them gamy old fellows and blindly followed their orders to jump overboard from training towers into a sea set afire with oil.

What most of my classmates dreaded were the long rowing hours, pulling on the oar of a lifeboat. For me, a day under a scorching sun in an open boat was a challenging adventure as I sat stripped to the waist, rowing with blistered hands along the steep shores, beaches and coves of war-time, deserted Catalina Island. I doted on this kind of training, and was put in charge of a boat. I was absolutely bloated with pride: my boat, my first command.

Among my most treasured mementos is the lifeboat certificate I earned at the training school, No. B305283. It hangs above my desk, faded and edge-torn, with the picture of myself pasted in one corner over a scene depicting a brave lifeboat crew pulling hard at their oars as their boat crests the wave of a stormy sea. It reads, in ponderous governmental prose:

> Samuel Donald McKinney, having proved to the satisfaction of the undersigned, designated by the Secretary of Commerce, that he has been trained in all the operations connected with launching lifeboats and the use of oars; that he is acquainted with the practical handling of the boats themselves and, further, that he is capable of understanding and answering the orders relative to lifeboat service, is hereby rated an efficient Lifeboat Man.

Sailor's knife in my pants, seabag over my shoulder and lifeboat certificate in my pocket, I graduated from the school and signed aboard my first ship, the SS *Devereaux*, as an acting able-bodied seaman. It was one of the Liberty ships, loaded with a cargo of grain for Italy. Just three days out from port, I realized that the maritime school had totally neglected to teach me the real trades of a merchant seaman which were drinking, fighting, chipping rust and painting.

One of my watchmates, Blackie, was a grinning, slightly crippled fellow with less than normal intelligence. He also slobbered. My other watchmate was a farm boy from North Dakota who had never seen a body of water larger than a prairie duck pond. His name was Keith and the two of us — as first-time-out beginners — had to endure the constant torments and threats hurled at us by the other members of the crew.

On the long, hot voyage down the coast of Central America, Keith and I slept on deck so that we could see the wonderful, star-filled nights of our southern passage. There, we shared our dreams. For Keith, the farm he would someday return to in North Dakota. For me, the sailboat I would someday own. Those dreams, those nights under the stars with the porpoises streaking along under the bows of the ship in shafts of phosphorescence, wrapped us in the magic of the sea — a reprieve from the sordid life below of oily heat, cockroaches and the constant, interminable complaints, brawls and boastful sexual recollections of the crew.

Ready to go to sea in the merchant marine.

Keith and I celebrated my 18th birthday in Panama City and returned to a ship gone mad, with the drunken, bloody crew hacking at each other with fire axes. Two of them were hospitalized and Keith and I had to stand double watches during the ship's transit of the canal. But then there was my first sunrise over the Atlantic after exiting the canal, followed by the nighttime beauty of the Windward Passage where I was able to read at midnight by moonlight as the ship crossed the moon-silvered Caribbean. And then there was Gibraltar, Spain and Europe on our left, Morocco and Africa on our right. Two continents in view and the ship leaving a clean, white wake across the blue Mediterranean. It was too many places at once, places I had known only on maps and in imagination. I was in a kind of geographical intoxication. I, just a riverboy, was on a ship passing through the portals of the Old World. It was an unforgettable landfall after an ocean crossing, a landfall that validated all my dreams of adventure.

As soon as the ship tied up in Genoa, Italy, the crew went ashore and stayed there for three days. Keith and I were the only deck crew left aboard to handle the ship's lines and assist the Italian stevedores in the unloading of the grain. We dutifully worked the clock around, sleeping when we could, as the unloading went on night and day. But duty, as the crew saw it, was to be with them in their absence from the ship. Drunk and furious they were when they returned and they tried to catch Keith and me to give us a beating. Had they caught us, they probably would have killed us, but Keith and I were able to run rings around those stumbling, bleary-eyed men who fell over themselves in their effort to teach us what merchant sailors were expected to do.

But the captain saw it differently and Keith and I were given leave for the rest of the time the ship was in port. I rented a bicycle and pedaled south to the lovely little necklace of towns on the Italian Riviera — Portofino, Rapallo and Santa Marguerite. This was after the end of World War II, and our ship was one of the first to arrive in peace-time Italy. In Portofino — much to my amazement — I was welcomed as a liberating Yank, a bicycle-riding sailor hero. I spent most of the month in Portofino, enjoying my war-hero status. Then, in the tradition of all sailors after a stay in port, I returned to my ship, surfeited with pleasures, broke and ready for the long voyage home.

It was a North Atlantic crossing in winter, that voyage back from Genoa to New York. The ship rolled and pitched and shook from bow to stern when the propeller lifted clear of the water. The watch on duty patrolled, looking for possible cracks in the deck. Many of the hastily built Liberty ships had suffered cracked plates in rough seas, so every time the ship hit the bottom of a wave trough and shouldered the mass of water in the next rising wave, we held tight to whatever was handy and waited for the sound of metal breaking apart.

After that trip to Italy, there were two intercoastal voyages: one from Seattle to New York, one from San Francisco to Baltimore. The crews were no different. The work was the same, chipping rust and painting, and the long, boring watches were monotonous. I had had a year as a merchant seaman, encountered some ocean storms, and had a few bruised knuckles as the mementos of a few unavoidable fights with men twice my size and age. The lure of a future career as a merchant sailor was beginning to fade. There was one last ship and on it a voyage I shall never forget.

CHAPTER FIVE

MY LAST SHIP

THE PORTLAND UNION HIRING hall (Sailors Union of the Pacific) assigned me to a ship ready to sail with a cargo of lumber from the Oregon port of Coos Bay. A quick replacement was needed for a crewman who had been injured. I took a train to Coos Bay, walked along the dock and found the ship.

It was the last of a breed, a squat little wooden ship of a type known along the West Coast as a "steam schooner" because it was the direct descendant of the old sailing schooners that used to haul lumber along the coast. It had an engine but that was about the only thing that made it a vessel of this century. Everything about it — I was soon to learn — was out of yesterday: the crew, the officers, the methods of navigation and the crew accommodations that were up forward in the bow of the ship in that traditional three-cornered hole known as the "fo'c's'le."

I stood on the dock examining this relic, now blowing black smoke from its single funnel in puffs as though ready and eager to get under way. The pilot house was aft, its windows like half-closed eyes, curving around it. A single wooden mast stood at the front end of the house with a single lifting boom attached to its base. Lines from the mast and boom led to two rusty winches on the deck. Forward of the house, and running almost to the point of the bow, was the cargo deck of the ship, stacked man-high with chained loads of long, yellow timbers. Red streaks from rusting bolts ran down the gray, scabby sides of the ship. No brass, no bright trim; just a dowdy old ship past its prime and kept from sinking, I thought, because all the lumber it carried would act like a huge, solid, wooden raft.

I was 18, a fully qualified able-bodied seaman, and pretty cocky. Along with my seabag, I carried a box of books and a small, portable typewriter. Loaded with all this literary baggage, I started up the gangway. From above me, a voice fell like a clap of thunder: "Where the hell do you think you're going with all that stuff?"

I looked up at the bridge and saw a large man — black pants, black shirt and black, peaked hat — leaning out over the rail, waiting for an answer.

"Sent down by the union. Said you were a man short."

"We are, but that ain't gonna be you with all that stuff."

But I knew he had to take me because ships had to take whomever the union sent them.

"I'll just stow this stuff forward out of sight," was the best reply I could make, and with that I stepped aboard, found an empty bunk in the fo'c's'le, and we left.

I don't remember any formalities of signing on. No crew member greeted me. I was not assigned to any watch. I was just there, the ship under way without whistle or fanfare. It chugged out of the harbor, met the easy swells of the Pacific, and turned south like a placid old plow horse following its way across a familiar field.

At dinner time, everyone gathered around a single table in the crew's mess room. Without a word, each man sat down at his place, his because he had sat there forever. When they were all seated, only one chair was vacant, mine, in the fixed order of some unspoken code. In front of me was a plate, a bowl and a cup but no silverware. None, anywhere on the table. Two men were slumped down in their chairs. Others, heads wobbling, moaned and groaned in what seemed to be some form of conversation back and forth across the table.

Then, in walked the steward with a gray enamel bucket of food that he placed on the table. He then returned to the galley and brought back a tray of bread. Back and forth he went, adding more pots and bowls to the table, and all the time his penis was hanging out and he was peeing on the deck. No one laughed, no one even noticed except me, my eyes wide with shock, horror and disgust as huge, meaty hands grabbed at food and pushed it with palm and fingers into open, slurping, burping mouths while the steward walked back and forth over the trail of his own urine.

I had two choices: I could get up and walk away from the table in disgust or I could eat my dinner. I looked around the table at the opening and closing mouths, smacking lips and soup-stained shirts, closed my fingers around a potato and shoved it into my mouth. As a feeble gesture of table etiquette, I licked each finger clean.

Dinner over, the men walked quietly forward to the fo'c's'le, crawled into their narrow, coffin-shaped bunks and fell asleep. I climbed up to the foredeck to look back at the pilot house. Behind closed windows, I could see a white face under the white hair of a short and very thin old man. His eyes seemed hollow, sightless; it was our helmsman, the captain himself. My God, I wondered, what have I gotten into on this relic of a ship manned by these silent, hoary old men?

The man who had hollered at me, I soon learned, was the first mate. He was an eagle, a hawk, in this ship of shuffling old gaffers. He was everywhere about the ship, a cursing rampage of orders and complaints that fell on deaf ears. Out of all of his crew, he had only one who jumped to his orders: me. On the second morning out, he ordered me over the side to paint the ship from a plank hung from the rail. Now painting, I knew, was a standard part of the work-day at sea but always this was done aboard the ship, not over the side. For two days, I hung outboard of that ship, painting gray over gray with only a plank between me and the gray sea below. On the third night of the voyage, we ran into a storm and the hanging plank was torn from the ship. The storm gave the mate other things to do, other men to holler at instead of me. The plank was not replaced and I was ignored on the gray ship that moved slowly down the coast on the cold, foggy voyage south.

At the end of a week, we tied up in the harbor of San Pedro, California, then a port city reckoned by merchant marine standards as one of the toughest in the world (Liverpool, England, it was claimed, was the toughest). The crew went to work unloading the vessel. Using hand-held hooks, they pulled individual boards and timbers together in stacks that were then lifted out of the ship and over to a dock by the single cargo boom. For some reason, I was not ordered to help at the unloading nor did any of the crew seem to want my help. They worked as though they were half asleep, slowly and silently, and board by board, the ship was unloaded.

The mate cursed their slowness, insulting them with every obscene allusion he could make that compared them with the low life forms of sea, whorehouse and gutter. The words fell off bent backs, without reply or response of any kind, just the dull thump of hooks being stuck into boards. At the end of the day's work, without washing, without a change of clothes, the crew went ashore, got drunk in the nearby bars and returned to the ship late in the evening as silently as they had left it.

We pulled out of San Pedro late one afternoon, the crew staggering drunk and sullen as they untied mooring lines and readied the now-empty ship for the sea. After we cleared the harbor, the mate gave the order to lower the long loading boom into its crutch on the foredeck. He supervised this operation by standing on the foredeck beneath the boom where he could guide it into place by shouting orders to the man at the winch and the men at the guy ropes who controlled the descent of the boom.

I was just standing by, watching the operation. Suddenly, there was a screech of cables running through blocks and the huge boom came crashing down on the foredeck. Instantly, the deck was deserted, all the crew scurrying into the fo'c's'le. Up on the bow, where the boom had landed, the mate lay sprawled on the deck. I ran to where he lay, expecting to find him dead. In jumping out of the way of the falling boom, he had stepped into the metal-ringed hawse hole and the calf of one leg had been nearly sliced off.

"Get me up," he screamed at me in fury and pain.

I lifted him to a sitting position, blood puddling around his foot.

"Hey, somebody, help me. Mate's been hurt," I hollered.

No response. I looked up to the pilot house, hollered again and pointed to the mate. I could see Old White Face up there, standing behind the wheel. His blank eyes just stared ahead, seeing nothing but the sea. This guy is going to bleed to death right here on the deck, I thought. I stomped on the deck with my feet, hoping to get the attention of the crew below. The puddle of blood widened, the mate no longer cursed, he just moaned, his hands clutching at his bent knee.

Jesus, what to do? Well, the obvious thing, of course: stop the bleeding. I straightened his leg and was able to roll his pants leg up to his knee, exposing the flap of skin and flesh hinged to his leg. I took off my shirt and wrapped it tightly around his calf, being careful to push the torn flesh back into place. I got him to his feet, took a heavy arm around my shoulder, and together we hobbled down the ladder, and across the deck to the foot of the stairs leading up to the next deck. Somehow, with me pushing and him pulling himself up the rails, we got up to the deck and then into his cabin where he fell into his bunk.

He was quiet — in shock, I assumed — so I unwrapped the leg to examine the slash. The bleeding was bad but there was no arterial pumping. I replaced my shirt with a tightly wrapped clean towel. After this very simple first-aid treatment for a wound that needed hospital stitching and care, I was at a loss to know what else I could do. The sensible thing would have been to turn the ship around and head back to port. The gray-ghost captain must have seen the accident, I assumed, and his decision had already been made. The ship was still steaming north.

My rudimentary knowledge of first aid had been acquired as part of the course that had earned me the lifeboat certificate, but that was all theory, and before me was a man who might bleed to death. I had not a friend aboard, nor — so it seemed — anyone who could help. It was the mate and me, a wounded man and an outcast, bound together by the blood slowly leaking from a massive leg wound. I sat in a chair in the mate's cabin, watching the expanding circle of blood darken the white towel. All I could do was try to keep him quiet, the compress of the towel tight, and wait.

He revived somewhat as I changed the towel. I told him I thought the bleeding was slowing, asked him if he was in great pain. All I got in response was a growl, like the growl of a large, wounded animal. After an hour or so, I went down to my bunk to get a book, knowing that I should keep a close watch over the mate for at least the remainder of the day. In the fo'c's'le, stinking of booze and vomit, the inert bodies of the crew lay in various poses of stupor after their big drunk in San Pedro. Open mouths snored and gurgled, limp arms pillowed heads, covered eyes or dangled from the bunks and swayed in the slow motion of the rolling ship.

Fog enclosed the vessel as it slowly plowed its way north through cold, damp days; a gray ship on a gray sea in a shroud of gray. Silent was the sea and silent the ship except for the steady, grinding throb of the propeller shaft and the rattle of the steering chain. I felt as though I was sailing backwards in time, that the fog-shrouded circle of our existence would never clear, and that someday I, too, would take my place among this sorry lot of aged ghosts padding silently back and forth between galley and bunks on slippered feet.

Twice each day I changed the bandage on the mate's leg. For two days he lay in his bunk without speaking, staring blankly at the cracked gray paint on the ceiling above his bed. Like a bear caged, he seemed cowed by his confinement, subdued because he was defenseless. He accepted my presence without a word until, on the third morning after the accident, he astounded me by asking for one of my books. I brought him a copy of Jack London's *Sea Wolf,* thinking that the brutal sealing-schooner captain, Wolf Larsen, would appeal to this hard, tough steam-schooner mate. I handed him the book, thinking he wanted to read it himself. But no, he handed it back to me with the command "Read it." He lay there in his bunk, his bloody leg propped up on a pillow, as I read, taking in every word, and now and then asking me to reread a particular paragraph which seemed to remind him of some previous experience.

For the rest of the passage, I bed-sat the mate, reading to him between his naps. I had almost finished the novel when we arrived off the mouth of Coos Bay. In the middle of a sentence, he held up his hand, told me to stop reading, and sat up. By some unerring instinct, he knew just where we were, got up, limped his way up to the pilot house, and took command of the ship as it started into the bay.

The next day I left the ship. As I was walking down the gangplank with my seabag, box of books and typewriter, the mate stopped me with almost the same words he greeted me with when I had first stepped aboard his ship.

"Where the hell you going now?"

"To college," I replied.

Then, almost embarrassed, he shook my hand and said very quietly, "Good place for you but remember — if you ever need a job, you have one if I still have a ship."

As I stood on the dock and watched him limp away, I was a very proud young sailor, saying goodbye to his last ship.

CHAPTER SIX

ALMOST TO TAHITI

CONTRARY TO THE MATE'S comment, college was not a good place for me. Certainly, I had much to learn and the desire to do so, but learning did not seem to be what college was for. Instead, I did what was expected of me: joined that bastion of post-adolescent clannishness called a fraternity, dated the right girls (so they told me), sipped whiskey out of paper bags at parties and tried to be one of the regular campus fellows. It all seemed rather silly and pointless.

What I did learn at college I learned by working on the school news-paper and I charted my studies toward a journalism degree. Short of graduation, I was offered the job of editor on a country weekly in a small town near Portland. I accepted; it paid $22.50 a week.

On that salary, I largely existed on the luncheons and dinners I attended as a reporter: Lions Club on Monday, Rotary on Wednesday, the Chamber of Commerce on Friday and Grange Hall pot lucks on the weekends. For a year and a half I worked on that paper. I was news editor, reporter, sports writer, photographer and editorial writer. What more could I want, I asked myself, believing I was on the threshold of an interesting career. I knew the answer to that question: I wanted to go big-boat sailing, ocean sailing. Big ambitions for a salary of 20 bucks a week.

I had been doing some small-boat racing with members of the Portland Yacht Club. One of them had an interest in a commercial fishboat he wanted to take south, and he asked me if I would like to go with him as crew.

With my total savings of $30, I headed south on the boat to Los Angeles where the owner sold it. From there, I hitch-hiked down the coast to Newport Beach, hoping that I would find a job of some sort on a sailboat. Newport Beach, then, was a small community and what there was of it largely centered around yachts that always needed painting or repairing.

At a cheap hotel — there were such things then in Newport Beach — near the entrance to the city fishing pier, a motherly manager let me have a room without advance payment. At night, I would sneak over the locked gate of the fishing pier, borrow one of the day-rent poles and catch a midnight supper that I cooked on the beach. In the morning, I would trade an hour of peeling potatoes for a breakfast. By the end of the week, I got a job scrubbing boat bottoms. It paid a dollar an hour, enough to cover my room rent and allow me to give up midnight fishing.

There were a number of young men like me who had come to this yachting center simply to sail and be around boats. For very little pay, we would do anything that needed doing on a boat: scrub, paint, rig, clean the bilges and climb the highest mast to replace a halyard. The money we earned was only to sustain us while we sought out what we really wanted: a bunk and free board as a crewman aboard a sailboat. Captain — as he liked to be called — Wes Bush saw me working in one of the boatyards and asked me if I would be interested in sailing with him to Tahiti in his 42-foot ketch, *Dubloon*.

Tahiti! It's where every sailor dreams of sailing, or at least it was one of my dreams. Man unknown, boat unseen, I answered him with an enthusiastic "YES!"

To make the cruise, the boat had to be painted, and all the rigging overhauled. I spent a fall and part of a winter working on *Dubloon*. Learned how to splice rope, sew canvas, make chafing gear and — the best part of it — sail a big boat that spread main and mizzen sails, two jibs, a staysail and a topsail. We did night sailing so that we were both familiar by touch with all the rigging. We worked out sail combinations for running, beating and heaving-to. Wes was a demanding skipper. Everything had to be done just right: no wrinkles in a furled sail, no lines left uncoiled, no dish, pan or tool ever out of place. Hard to please, he was, but willing to teach me and what we were doing together was preparing for that long-distance sail to Tahiti so I had no complaints.

Beyond getting to know each other and the way of the boat, there was another reason for our frequent coastal voyages: to intro-

Aboard Dubloon.

duce Wes's bride, Sybil, to sailing and — he hoped — to get her to enjoy it so that she would look forward to the Tahiti cruise. We cruised to all the offshore California islands and to Santa Barbara and San Diego. We had lavish dinners ashore at marinas, drinks in the harbor of Catalina Island and sun-filled days of easy sailing, and Sybil seemed to be enjoying it all. Even her dog, Tuppence, a fat female cocker spaniel, no longer whined and cowered when the boat began to heel.

So all was well aboard *Dubloon.* Skipper and crew got along. The boat, with its freshly painted black hull, new rigging, and twin gaff-headed sails, was the picture of what a long-distance cruising boat should look like on the eve of a departure for the South Seas. The bride was enjoying herself, the dog had found places where she could hide when things got tippy. Tahiti — I thought — was just over the horizon.

And then came the storm. A vicious one that blew up almost without warning one afternoon as we were sailing back from one of the islands. It caught us with all plain sail up, main, mizzen and jib. The lee rail went under as Wes fought to turn the boat into the wind. Over, over, and over the boat heeled, water spilling into the cockpit. Tuppence was trying to crawl her way to the high side of the deck, her claws frantically scratching for holds in the deck seams. Sybil stared with horror at the ocean water that was supposed to be outside the boat, not in it, and ran for the security of the cabin. I was helping her back down the companionway ladder when Wes hollered, "Fuck that god-damned woman and get the mainsail down!"

I did as my captain ordered me: pushed Sybil down through the hatch, threw her dog on top of her, banged the hatch shut and went forward to drop the main. All night Wes and I fought to keep the boat off the lee shore. Just after dawn we were able to enter the security of Newport Beach and tie the boat to its dock. I opened the hatch. Out charged Sybil, shaking with anger.

"I shall never forget what you said to me, Wes Bush, and I'll never set foot on this boat again." With that she stomped ashore and with her went our cruise to Tahiti.

CHAPTER SEVEN

SHIPWRECKED IN MEXICO

INSTEAD OF SAILING TO Tahiti, I sailed to Mexico on the 82-foot ketch *Maggie*, a boat well past its prime as was its skipper, Jiggs. Improvisations — making do with what could be scrounged — was how both stretched out their lives: *Maggie* to stay afloat, Jiggs to turn a few dollars as a charter-boat skipper fishing for marlin in the Gulf of California. His partner in this enterprise was a man named Black Bart. I, still the book-toting romantic, a dandified "yachtie" by the measure of these two men, was dubbed "Sir Cedric."

So, off we went, Jiggs, Black Bart and Sir Cedric in the leaking old *Maggie*, bound for La Paz in Baha, Mexico, where the fortunes of all four of us were to be enriched by wealthy sportsmen who would fly down to join us.

"Money practically in the bank," Jiggs would exclaim as he rubbed his hands together and danced the little three-step hop that had earned him his name. "And all we have to do is reel in the fish while Cedric baits the hooks and pours drinks." Sir Cedric, I began to realize as we sailed south, would have a number of important duties aboard *Maggie*: bartender, cook, dishwasher, steward and — when not otherwise occupied — sail trimmer, helmsman, and fish-spotter.

With such a good, all-around crewman-flunky as Sir Cedric, Jiggs was able to devote himself to the two electrical systems of the boat that were his creation and his obsession: a huge refrigeration system and a radio that could talk to the world.

The refrigeration system served as a deep-freeze for steaks and as a source of ice; luxuries, of course, reserved for the paying guests who would come aboard in La Paz. The electrical challenge was to keep the deep-freeze at freezing temperature in the heat of Mexico. Two auxiliary engines, one banging away 24 hours a day and the other on stand-by, supplied current for both the freezer and the radio. They also supplied power for the fans which were placed below deck to cool the interior of the ship and thus reduce the power demand of the refrigerator system.

In theory, it was a good plan, if the system had been designed for the job and if the components worked. Jiggs's electrical system had none of these virtues. It was something he had put together out of odd parts, house wire, automobile batteries and discarded switches and fuse boxes. Wires went everywhere: through bulkheads, across ceilings, under floorboards and through cupboards. The control panel of this spider's web of electrical lines was lodged exclusively in the electrical memory circuits of Jiggs's brain. Black Bart and I walked below decks at night with flashlights, afraid that if we turned on a switch we would be in conversation with some ham operator in Tierra del Fuego.

Jiggs was everywhere about the boat day and night, armed with pliers, fuses and circuit testers as he tried to control power outages, short circuits and hot wires. And when he worked at night, he liked to hear the radio reports from the far corners of the world which were carried throughout the boat by a series of relay speakers, broadcasting incomprehensible conversations at high, squeaky volume. Oh yes; I remember those moon-drenched nights sailing down the coast of Baha: the land a dark silhouette across the silvered wrinkles of the seas and the old *Maggie,* generators banging away, fans whirring and radio blaring, cutting a noisy swath through the soft, warm night.

It was Black Bart who made the daily passages pleasant for me because he insisted on sailing whenever possible. The *Maggie*, with her huge spread of sail, her long hull and shallow underbelly, could really get up and go on a downwind run. But it was the economy of sailing, not the thrill of it, that appealed to Black Bart. Wind was free; gasoline for the engine was not, so whenever possible, we sailed.

Black Bart's role in this enterprise was never made clear to me. Jiggs owned the boat and it appeared — from what I could hear — that Black Bart was financing the operation. It must have been a lean one because he growled at the amount of gas burned, the portions of food served and the amount of paint and varnish Sir Cedric used to keep the old *Maggie* in some form of presentable cosmetic appearance.

Halfway down the coast, we put in at Magdalena Bay, then an absolute nothingness of hot, dry shores surrounding a bay teeming with spouting whales and leaping manta rays. It seemed, as we sailed into the bay, that there was just not room enough for the boat, the whales and the huge manta rays that heaved and flopped in the entry channel. There was no settlement of any kind in the bay but on one point stood the deserted try-works of an old whaling factory. The beach was littered with the white, bleached bones of whale skeletons and the old iron pots used for melting blubber. Because Baha was so dry, these relics of another time were perfectly preserved as though the works had been abandoned only yesterday.

And we fished; my lord, what fishing there was in that bay. More than the three of us could ever eat at one meal, so we cut the fish into strips, hung them in the rigging to dry, and served them in a sauce of tequila and lime juice. The lobster tails we boiled and then piled on platters like apples in a pyramid.

A few days later we rounded Cabo San Lucas and anchored off the small town of San Jose del Cabo. Today, the town is a highly developed tourist destination. When I was there in the *Maggie*, it was a tiny village surrounded by sugar cane fields, its one road unpaved. A few adobe and tile houses surrounded the main plaza but most of the Mexicans lived in palm-thatched huts. The only vehicles in town were a few ancient trucks used to haul sugar cane.

We anchored, rowed ashore in the dinghy, walked a dirt path into town and were met by the mayor who came out to greet the rarity of visiting yachtsmen. He showed us around the town and then invited us to play golf with him. Golf consisted of the mayor, three clubs, six golf balls and a group of small boys who chased the balls we drove down the street from the main plaza. That was San Jose del Cabo in 1949, the last port of call for the *Maggie*.

Two days later, the boat sank in Los Muertos Bay, a few miles south of La Paz. We arrived in the bay a little after dark, all of us very tired. Without spending too much time nosing around for a good anchorage, we just dropped the hook and went to bed. The boat's anchoring system was another of Jiggs's inventions: an old B-29 landing-gear motor that served as a winch, and a frayed length of cable. Sometime during the night, a strong offshore wind came up. Either the anchor dragged or the cable parted but once free of the bottom, the boat sailed out of the harbor, hit a rock and sank.

All of us were asleep below deck. We heard a thump, something like a huge mallet smashing through the bottom of the boat, and in the next second the cabin was waist-deep in water. We jumped for the ladder and climbed frantically to the deck to avoid being trapped below. The boat just sank under us as we stood there wondering what had happened. Calmly, quietly and standing straight up, the old girl just disappeared beneath us. We didn't even have to dive overboard; when there was no boat under us to stand on, we just swam to the shore. We crawled out on the beach, wordless in the aftershock. One minute we were sleeping, and in the next minute we were standing on the beach, barefoot, nearly naked, no boat in sight.

"Shoes!" said Black Bart. "How can we walk anywhere in this country without them?"

Again I point out that this was Baha in the late 1940s, essentially roadless and unsettled. La Paz, the nearest and only city, was a long walk north: hot, dry, and waterless. We could *die* here was the unspoken thought that filled our minds.

The night was warm and the hot day a few hours away. We sat on the beach staring at the place where the *Maggie* had sunk, still mentally numbed, hoping the impossible, that she might rise up out of the water or that the dinghy might float free of the boat. But the *Maggie* was gone and everything with her. What might have floated free was blown out to sea by the offshore wind.

We were wrecked, castaway and stranded. That was how the dawn found us and how a lone fisherman traveling up the coast found us; three naked men standing on a beach with no boat in sight was something to investigate. Juan did so, took us aboard and carried us to La Paz.

Jiggs was known in La Paz because he had been there before in the *Maggie*. That familiarity made it easy for him and Black Bart to register at a hotel and get a new outfit of clothes. Sir Cedric was left to fend for himself, shoeless and penniless in a foreign Mexican town. But not for long because it was Mexico, a place of poor people but people generous with what little they had.

Juan the fisherman invited me to stay with him, his wife, Juanita, and their three children in his grass hut at the edge of town. I could offer them nothing; he asked for a like amount. The hut had a dirt floor. My guest bed was a pile of straw, shared when I was not there by chickens. The three lovely children watched my every move with huge, brown eyes. Juanita was small, very pretty, with her black hair braided down her back, and she sang to herself as she kneeled to pound out tortillas on a flat stone.

But how to get out of La Paz? No boats were heading north and the road connecting La Paz with California was rarely traveled. I was told that a small freighter made weekly runs to Mazatlan across the gulf and though the passage cost only a few pesos, I had not a peso in my pocket.

Somehow — I can't recall the chain of events — I got a job in a boatyard, then building and repairing fishboats. I was hired as a painter for the specialized job of painting the boot-top stripe along the waterline of a boat. I laugh today when I think of that job; it gave me the title of "maestro" and a young boy to hold my paint bucket as I artfully applied that line to a boat.

I worked there for a week or so — just long enough to buy a ticket on the freighter — and came home each evening to sit with Juan and his family outside their little hut, surrounded by other Mexican families living under palm trees by the bay. It was wonderfully peaceful there, the ageless scene of men resting after a day's work, the musical conversation of women cooking and children playing. I felt that I had come to the end of something, that the water trails I had been following had brought me to this little community of men, women and children, and that it was now time to go home. And so I did, and years were to pass before I returned to the sea.

CHAPTER EIGHT

NORTHWEST WATERS

I N A FEW YEARS of knocking around as a sailor, I had learned a fair amount about boats and ships. What I had not learned was that the most dangerous part of a sailor's life was not the sea but the shore. And so it was the shore that grounded me after my return from Mexico; grounded me for years on the reefs of marriage, fatherhood, four children and a job. Along the way, a varied career as a newspaper reporter, copy writer for an advertising agency, development director for a private school and, lastly — one worth doing — director of a college Outward Bound-type program. Then a floundering marriage, a divorce and, at age 45, I left my job at the college and essentially had to begin all over again. What to do? I had no desire to return to anything similar to what I had been doing. Wanted something not in an office, wanted to produce something other than paper files. Did not want to go to meetings, listen to office gossip, watch the clock waiting for five P.M., count the days to Friday.

Go back, I said to myself, back to something you loved, something you were, something never wholly completed. Back to what you learned in that rowboat on the river, that fishing village of your youth, that job as a deckboy on the sternwheeler. Find something that will take you back to the river and the sea. And so I built a boat.

The boat I built was a dory, a descendant of that humble craft of legend and utility that was developed in the last century for cod fishing off the Grand Banks of Newfoundland. The distinctive shape of the dory — the swoop and lift of its sheer, sharply angled sides and tombstone-shaped transom — is an icon of maritime art and literature. Neither time, nor chipped paint nor scabby planks can mar the perfection of that shape. See a dory pulled up on a beach or moored to some back corner of a dock and its very presence is an unspoken story told in strands of fish line caught in bottom boards, a rusty bailing can, and the dead leaves and grasses of some distant shore brought home as mementos of voyages past.

For a long winter, I was a basement recluse as I built that boat, a voluntary exile from the upstairs pleasures of my new wife, our friends, good food, warmth and ordered living. Alone, in that solitary task of building, I had to confront my doubts and my lack of skill. What carried me from fumbling to learning, from hesitancy to courage, was the passionate anticipation of having a boat that could return me to the sea. The hard part was the discipline to be patient during the long sequence of putting together the many parts and pieces that form the collective whole of a boat.

Not much of a boat, that little open dory, just 20 feet long. It had two sails, a five-horsepower outboard and a back-up set of oars. The bottom of the boat was the bunk, a brass-bound box was the galley. Minimal but enough for where I wanted to sail it, which was along the west coast of Vancouver Island in British Columbia.

Along that coast, the land meets the Pacific as a broken shore of islands and reefs, deep sounds and inlets. A place of space, time, light and life is this wild coast, staggering in its beauty. Islands loom everywhere, their contours shaped by wind and wave and softened by the damp wash of fog and sea mist or lit by a setting sun followed by a sky of stars. The sea sets the mood of the coast, surging as endless waves along the outside shores, quiet and calm in the long, protected inlets. And everywhere there is life; life that swims in the sea, clings to rocks, leaves footprints along sandy beaches and lofts on the wind.

During one long summer, I explored that coast in the little dory, from Barkley Sound in the south to Nootka Island in the north. It was then a mostly roadless coast, as yet largely untouched by commercial logging, a last wilderness of sea and forested shores. My voyage had no particular destination. Just being wherever time and chance carried me was the order of each day as I slowly followed close along curving shorelines of rock, beach or forest, and crossed open, sun-burnished channels of the sea to disappear again into the sheltered lagoons of encircling islands. Wildlife was my company: mink, river otter, deer, bear, eagles in the tops of old snags and sea gulls by the thousands. In the sea, along rocky shores and reefs, in tide pools and in underwater grottos of waving green, brown and red weed, life existed in staggering abundance. In places, huge sea urchins blanketed the sea bottom, pin-cushions of purple scavenging for food. At low tides, rocks were ringed by massive clusters of intertwining starfish, their arms purple, orange, yellow and red.

In a small body of water enclosed by three of the Barkley Sound islands, I saw seals herding salmon. Splashing and diving, they encircled the school, driving them into a vortex of frantic fish trying to escape capture. One by one and in turn, a seal would dive into the center of the mass, grab a salmon, and then rejoin the herding circle.

In the quiet channels of the Pinkerton Group, I watched antlered deer swimming from island to island, was startled by a bear slapping a fish from a small creek and sat for hours watching the otter in their game of tag along the edge of the shore.

Many nights I would anchor the boat and then wade ashore to camp on the outreach of a sandy spit, one man, alone, in the sunset gathering of the birds. In the cove on Turret Island, I dug in the grass-covered midden of an ancient Indian village, poked with a

The dory, anchored in Barkley Sound, British Columbia.

stick through the layers of a thousand village meals. A quiet place was that cove, topped by that midden and while I was sitting there, a strange thing happened. A voice I could not hear asked me to leave the island. Now I am not superstitious, nor do I believe in spirits, and so this voice — or whatever it was — I ignored. Until it asked again that I should leave. And I did.

Why did I obey that voice? Well, perhaps because the west coast is so completely a place of untamed sea and forested wilderness, where creatures of land and sea engage in the constant tooth-and-claw drama of survival; perhaps because of these things, the human visitor with civilized fetishes and habits begins to think and act in more elementary ways. As I did when I obeyed the voice.

The encounter with the orcas, more than anything, stripped away that superior human perspective by which I viewed the world. One evening as I was quietly sailing through one of the Barkley Sound inlets, the stillness was suddenly shattered by the explosive blowing of a pod of killer whales that rose out of the water to surround me on both sides. Eye level to eye level, I traveled for a few minutes among those beautiful animals with glistening white and black bodies, and during those moments, it seemed as though we had established some form of mental contact with each other across the water.

With one swipe of a tail, I could have been destroyed, but there was a kind of fatalistic thrill for me in traveling with a group of animals who were in charge of the encounter. They could have made a murderous charge or simply disappeared. Instead, we continued together for some distance down the channel, each of us very aware of the other. They, not I, were the superior life in this sea: perceptive, intelligent and curious about the creature called man who traveled with them.

Another day, farther north along the coast off Nootka Island, the course of the dory intercepted the path of a group of migrating gray whales. They were huge, monstrous shapes that suddenly rose up out of the deep, oblivious to an encounter with a small boat which, to them, was probably only a spot on the surface of the sea. Their great bodies were scarred and mottled, and in the plume of their released breath was the smell of deep ocean. I watched them with a sense of profound awe and felt through those beasts a connection with a primordial life, a million years of oceanic migrations, mating and death.

There was then a man living in a floathouse on that coast, a man who, though totally uneducated, intuitively understood those connecting experiences with the natural world that I have tried to describe.

He was known as Salal Joe and he was referred to as the "hermit of Barkley Sound." Where he came from was a mystery. Some thought Joe an Arab, a Pole, or an escapee from the Russian army. Certainly, there was something in his past that had frightened Joe, something he seemed to be running from. He was tall, dark and bearded, and he had piercing eyes that at times darted arrows of hostility, at other times showed looks of innocence and wonder.

He lived in a one-room shack on a float covered with neat stacks of firewood, mounds of rope and miscellaneous flotsam of the sea.

Joe had built rows of planter boxes from salvaged lumber, and in these boxes he grew beans, root vegetables, flowers and spindly trees. His only companion was a cat named Checo. His boat, a small rowboat he had built, was named *Hello Nature.*

The boat's name, as I got to know Joe, was the key to his personality, the explanation for his life as a recluse. When I heard that his boat had been found upside down on one of the island beaches, I knew Joe was dead. It released me from a promise I had made to him never to write about him while he was alive.

It took quite a few visits and a lot of rum before Joe would talk about his life. He was no misanthrope. On the contrary, it was the burden of sadness he carried for the human race that had driven him to his lonely exile on the coast.

Where he lived, and how he lived, were inarticulate expressions of the rage he felt for the killing of life in all its forms.

He spoke with a very broken accent and sometimes, after we had listened on his shortwave radio to reports of war and violence, he would turn to me and say, "Vy do ve do dat to each other?" The taking of life — life in any form — was such a terrible thing to Joe that he had cut himself off from the world so he would not have to participate in any forms of killing.

In addition to the garden boxes on his float, Joe had planted fruit trees on some of the islands. I assumed he planted them for himself but no, he never ate what he grew: it was all for the "leetle creatures," the deer, birds and small animals of the islands. It was the caring for these creatures that sustained him in his lonely life, a kind of payment he could make for all the killing that took place in the world.

I thought of him as the Saint Francis of the islands, a man who would get hell-roaring drunk on anything potable, then go out in his boat at midnight to watch the moonlight reflecting off the scales of a thousand migrating fish. In the middle of a conversation he would stop talking, cock his head and say, "Hear dat? He's calling." From out of the night noises of wind and the distant surf, he would recognize the call of an owl. He would be expecting it. He knew the owl's tree, its habits and its cycles. Each night he waited for its call, a living voice talking to him from somewhere out there in the dark.

Innocence and despair; the two are not often mated in the psyche of one man. At some time, at some place in Joe's life, he had worked on a farm. He described it as a huge, flat plain, covered by tiny, bright-green blades of grass.

"Back and forth went those huge machine, pounding the tiny grasses to dust," he would say, rolling his hands and arms like wheels. "Back and forth till everything gone." And then, angrily, "You tell me Sam, vy dey do dis to leetle blades of grass no bigger than my finger? Vy?"

Joe knew there was no answer; all he could do was to try to take care of the life around him with the trees and plants he grew. This he did because of what he believed, a belief he summed up in the simple statement that was his creed: "Sam, you got to put zomzing back."

Life, not death, was in that simple statement and so he lived in a self-imposed exile with his cat and the creatures of the island as he tended his island gardens. One lone man's effort to "put something back."

The memory of my voyage is its journal, the brief, hastily written entries that record scenes, events and impressions. I do not edit them; the immediacy of their words contains the sense and conditions in which they were written, with one hand holding a pencil, the other hand on the tiller.

Notes from the Log:
Morning cool under a sun becoming hot. Slowly drifting and sailing along an island shore, close enough to almost feel the rocks turn and swell and shape themselves into various forms. Herons, seals and birds watch my slow progress with curious but apprehensive eyes. Each rock, animal, each bird is where it belongs. I am the intruder here trying — wanting — to become a part of this place of shore and sea.

Anchor for lunch in a small cove, then wade ashore and walk up the rock-terraced shore. What a change when I step from sea to shore, from a boat always in motion, to the rigidity of stone. Up here on the terraces, everything is wind-twisted, gnarled and spiky stiff in its reach for the sun. Below me, like a weightless sea-forest, floats a ring of seaweed, its delicate, wet and glistening fronds yielding to the gentle surge of the sea.

Cove watching at dawn with nothing and everything to see. A rising sun back-lights the mountains and then, when it comes up, light spills down the valleys and reaches out across the sea to touch the island with a new day while a full moon hangs like an out-of-place orb in the blue sky. Then out around Wower, the outermost island, past rocks where huge bull sea lions bellow at the intrusion of a passing boat. The sea is covered in foam from waves breaking against rocks, so thick that it muffles the sound of the engine, as I ride up and over the white-frothed swells, like mounded hills of snow.

I was a month traveling that coast in that tiny dory. Rain, heat, wind and the long daylight hours, the missed meals and my cramped sitting position at the tiller had become my life and I wanted no other. I found myself taking great delight in the smallest of occurrences: the simplicity of washing my dishes over the side of the boat in a sink hundreds of feet deep; my afternoon ritual of donning my salt-stained blue jacket for a rum drink as the boat floated over the great depths of the sea like a shadow on a blue skin of water.

Every day, I awoke before dawn with an intense sense of anticipation. Another day had come around for exploring places I had never seen. The pleasure lay in just following wherever the sea channels and island contours led, sometimes in shadows beneath cliffs, sometimes in the sunlight of open water. In that mood, I felt I could have gone on forever, as though boat and I could travel on and on, existing on nothing more than light and air. I had to remind myself to eat; sleep was what I did when it became too dark to travel.

My voyage along the coast ended north of Nootka Island on a trio of little islands connected to each other at low tide by a narrow strand of sand. I named them Winken, Blinken and Nod. A steep, rocky trail led me to the summit of Winken where I sat down in a tiny meadow sprinkled with wildflowers and moss-covered rocks mottled with yellow splotches of lichen.

I crossed over to Blinken and walked through the shoulder-high brush that crowned its summit, an island forest for one tiny browsing deer. Around Nod's diminutive shoreline, deep rock pools contained goblets of clear water left by the retreating tide. Small sea anemones ringed the edges of these sea bowls and tiny crabs and fish scurried for shelter as my shadow fell across the pools. Each step over a pebbled beach of ocean-polished stones and shells revealed other small creatures that crawled, dug, or squirted at my approach, each burrow, tunnel or crevice an island of life within an island.

I returned to the summit of Winken and sat down. I had picked up a walking stick from the beach and, sitting there, I began carving little notches on it as I listened to sounds amid silence. Time, as a conscious thing, seemed to disappear. My stick began to be patterned with more elaborate cuttings. Did the end of the forked branch look like an eagle? Was the knot the eye of a seal?

I left the island and returned to the boat, then watched as the tide flooded the strand and washed away my footprints. The carved stick I left behind on the summit of Winken, my totem to watch over that immensity of sea, land and sky until I could return.

CHAPTER NINE

ISLANDS

I RETURNED THE NEXT year with the dory to explore the vast maze of islands lying in the waters of the Strait of Georgia and Queen Charlotte Strait between the British Columbia mainland and Vancouver Island. Of all geographical forms, I find islands — those pieces of land surrounded by water and the need for a boat — the most intriguing. I am not alone in the enjoyment of that disease writer Lawrence Durrell — an old islander himself — called "islomania."

Islands are places apart, geographically and philosophically separate from all other places. They seem to be enwrapped within their own laws and sense of time. One look at an island across a stretch of water and most people feel the desire to land there. Islands seem to offer something missing from the mainland, something people might be seeking: a brief escape from the routine and artifices of mainland life, an engagement with the simple but immutable natural laws of an island and the possibility of encountering something called "adventure."

Islands, in their wholeness and integrity, "belong to a different time," wrote anthropologist Loren Eiseley, "something not quite in simultaneous relationship with the rest of the world." An island has the power to draw a person outward to a contemplation of things larger than himself, in comradeship with solitude and the timeless rhythm of a natural order.

Throughout Western literature, islands have stood as dramatic settings for adventures, noble deeds and skulduggery. Defoe, Twain, Melville, Stevenson, London, Maugham, Michener, Durrell — these authors placed some of their most colorful characters and exciting stories in island settings, there to deal, in isolation and insularity, with themes and stories that touch on all the emotions and dreams and ambitions of human life.

The islands I wanted to explore in those northern waters had their own stories to tell, the stories of the ancient island inhabitants, the hunter-gatherers of a generous land and sea which they harvested with an elaborate technology of wood, stone and bone. It was a culture that some 2,500 years ago reached its full development and then changed very little because its technologies and traditions were in perfect harmony with the natural world of the sea and forest that sustained them.

I tried to imagine a millennium of silence on these islands, broken only by the sound of the sea, the howl of the wind, the squawk of the raven, and the splash of the salmon. These were the only sounds heard by the native people of these island shores, while Alexander's army swept across Persia, while Christian martyrs screamed in the Colosseum of Rome, while Vikings shouted war cries as they invaded Great Britain. Still silence for these people as Columbus began the maritime exploration of the New World, an exploration that 286 years later would see a ship drop anchor off Vancouver Island's west coast and the silent world of these people forever changed.

But the beauty of their islands remains largely the same. Over them hangs a canopied sky that is much of the time a misty gray, sometimes wind-rent and sometimes of a clean, sparkling clarity that makes the island clusters stand out like pieces of uncut jade. And, they are still places mostly of silence.

I trailered the boat to Vancouver, launched it in English Bay, and headed westward through the Strait of Georgia toward Lasqueti Island, 36 miles west from Vancouver. Very carefully, I steered the boat through the narrow, rock-edged slot at the southern end of the island that opened to the tiny harbor of Squitty Bay and tied up at the government dock.

Lasqueti fits Loren Eiseley's idea of an island as "something not quite in simultaneous relations with the rest of the world." I stayed there for two days, walking again and again to the point to listen to the wind and the ever-constant sound of the sea breaking on the rocks outside the harbor. And I listened to the island people who wandered down to the dock and talked with me. Each sound — wind, sea and island voice — seemed to be saying something, that Lasqueti was a very special place, a place that moved with the rhythms of natural and human life in tune with each other to produce what islander Lawrence Durrell called a "landscape of the heart."

It is a landscape that called me to quiet study of an overhanging tree, a flower-sprinkled meadow, and the contentment expressed by the man I saw slowly, artfully, shingling a cabin roof. Those islanders on Lasqueti I met and talked with seem to be hearing what their landscape is saying, and they are responding to it by trying not to impose too much of themselves on it. One man showed me the small electrical-generating system he had made by placing a tin-can waterwheel in a small creek. I admired a lovely little sailboat of masterful craftsmanship tied up next to my boat on the dock. Admired it even more when its owner told me he had built it with hand tools from lumber washed up on the beach.

For one night, I, too, was a resident of Lasqueti. I had gone ashore with only a sleeping bag to sleep out on one of the points. Sitting there, I thought that of all places in the world where I would like to have a house, this would be it. And so, drawing with a stick in the sand, I laid out the plan of a one-room house. A living-room corner that would look south over the strait; a bedroom in the eastern corner to get morning sunlight; kitchen looking west to the high mountains of Vancouver Island; the blank side of the house a wall for books and pegs for clothing, fishing poles and rain gear.

A perfect house, that one-room cabin I slept in that night on the rock- and madrona-clad tip of Lasqueti Island, open to the wind and sun of fair weather, battened and closed to winter storms. In the morning, I erased its lines from the sand and sailed away from the island.

It was an unimportant objective, one of curiosity, that took me up Agamemnon Channel to Jervis Inlet to pass over the 2,214-foot depth of water at the northern tip of Nelson Island. I tried to imagine the dark depth of water beneath the quarter-inch skin of my boat and felt the curious sensation of floating on the surface of water nearly a half-mile deep.

Looking at the chart as I drifted over that watery abyss, I studied the names of the nearby islands and waters, and saw that I was surrounded by a dimension more interesting than a hole in the water: a dimension of history. The surrounding place names all related to the historic 1805 Battle of Trafalgar in which British ships destroyed Napoleon's Franco-Spanish fleet.

Nelson Island was named for Horatio Nelson, the one-eyed, one-armed admiral who commanded the victorious fleet. Agamemnon Channel, through which I had sailed, carries the name of the first line-of-battle ship Nelson commanded. The *Agamemnon* was also the sixth ship behind Nelson's *Victory* to break the line of the Franco-Spanish fleet.

Jervis Inlet, to the north of Nelson Island, was named for John Jervis who, as the Earl of St. Vincent and First Lord of the Admiralty, saw Nelson as a captain of great promise: he gave him the rank of commodore, and command at the centers of conflict leading up to the Battle of Trafalgar.

Hardy Island carries the name of Vice-Admiral Sir Thomas Hardy who, as flag captain of the *Victory*, saw Nelson shot and killed by a French sharpshooter. And Cape Cockburn, where I anchored for the night, was named for the man who commanded the ship that took Napoleon to his prison on St. Helena — Admiral Sir George Cockburn.

Names bestowed on places in these waters are a mix of myth, religion, topographical descriptions, personal vanities, crew members or officers, pioneer settlers, national leaders, heroes, patrons and saints.

Of particular interest to me were the names left by the Spanish, English and American explorations of the late 18th and early 19th centuries. Long, difficult and hazardous were those voyages along the coasts of these northern lands and, with each mile charted and each place named, a small addition was made to bring a piece of an unknown world into the orbit of the known. A name left behind by one of these voyages was a place fixed in geography that could be returned to on a later journey by sea or land, a place no longer unknown.

I think of these chart names as the name-prints of history. More than just the names of geographical places, they tell the history and story of a place.

Names bestowed by the native people are interesting because they grew out of a direct experience with the landscape. It might be a name connected with a legend, but more often a name was related to the natural features of a place or the food that could be gathered at that place.

To know those Indian names, and to understand and respect them, is to know something about the culture that bestowed them. Take away those names of a people, rip them out of their language, and they are left with only memories. And this was done to these people, writes historian James Ronda. The taking of names "out of a native context," he writes, "and redefining ... in European terms ... is a kind of imperial kidnapping, a cultural hijacking that remade the country."

George Vancouver, in his 1792 circumnavigation of Vancouver Island, bestowed 75 names that honored English royalty, admirals and prominent men of his expedition. All the names he bestowed on his survey of the inland sea remain on the charts today. Spanish place names — Galiano, Texada, Malaspina, Quadra, Redonda and others — are a reminder that these waters and surrounding lands were once considered possessions of the Spanish Crown.

In the process of assigning to these places European names, most of the original Indian names were discarded. But I don't charge those men who renamed the coastal places with a kind of etymological genocide. It was, I think, their very human reaction to being in places new to them. They were, in the most profound sense, explorers. They had sailed over the rim of the known and were probing the unknown. Exciting, this sense of discovery, yes, but also disturbing for these explorers roaming about strange, uncharted places. By scattering names along such a shore, they brought it into the comforting orbit of the known.

Barry Lopez, writing from the perspective of the Arctic vastness, touches on this idea of converting space into a sense of place. He writes,

> We turn these exhilarating and sometimes terrifying new places into geography by extending the boundaries of our old places in an effort to include them. We pursue a desire for equilibrium and harmony between our familiar places and unknown space. We do this to make the foreign comprehensible, or simply more acceptable.

Another destination of curiosity was Mitlenatch Island in the Strait of Georgia where the tides meet. This occurs because the tidal front sweeps into the waters behind Vancouver Island from two directions. From the north, it flows down through Queen Charlotte Strait and Discovery Passage; from the south, it runs in from the Strait of Juan de Fuca, and then turns north through the Strait of Georgia. The two tidal fronts meet off Mitlenatch.

There is nothing dramatic about the encounter, no swirling waters or wild currents; the two flooding tides just meet and turn away from each other to run back in the opposite directions of their ebbs. If the pilot of a boat were to calculate the tides just right, he could travel north on the north-moving flood, wait for the change, then continue north, still traveling with a north-flowing tide.

As one travels up the coast, Lund is the last town on the mainland shore of southern British Columbia. There, the highway stops and that alone is reason enough to go to Lund. It is one of the few places in the world of today where the automobile trail comes to an end. Beyond Lund only the boatman can go.

But the "Lundites" claim that their town is not the end of the road, but the beginning of the long Trans-American Highway that leads south through Canada, the United States, Mexico, and Central and South America.

Northward from Lund is Desolation Sound, gateway to a seascape of thousands of islands, rocks and reefs, tide races, and fiords leading to mountain glaciers, waterfalls and wild places where still live bear, cougar and wolf. A last meal at a sit-down restaurant, fuel and water tanks filled, and toward this horizon of exploration I headed.

I entered those waters through Homfray Channel, the curving arc of a glacier-carved sea canyon that swallowed me in its vastness as I headed north out of Desolation Sound. I paused off Booker Point on East Redonda Island and tilted my head backwards to look up at the 5,000-foot summit of Mount Addenbroke.

Waterfalls dropped from the misty heights of the Pryce Channel shoreline. Not the lacy falls of the artist's landscape painting, these falls, but the tumbling violence of falling water, gouging and tearing at the land, uprooting trees and washing out rock in its vertical drop to the sea. The noise was that of freight trains rumbling above the cloud-draped slopes. Farther along the channel, another waterfall dropped from the sky like a twisting rope of white water that exploded in spray and fell to the sea in soft, scalloped patterns that formed a curtain of froth down the face of the cliff.

The sight of a church steeple pulled me in from Calm Channel to a walk around Church House Bay. This little community is now deserted, its few remaining houses trashed and overgrown, windows broken. The interior of the church had been stripped of all religious symbols with the exception of one small stained-glass window, its sacred motif sparing it from the desecration of hurled stones. I stood on the fallen porch of that church on a Sunday morning, looking at the neglected dock and the houses, now vacant and returning to the loam of the shore. What might it have looked like many years ago, I wondered, with people arriving in boats from other coastal communities to gather on the beach, to exchange gossip, to walk the hillside path up to the church and there to sit together as a community of worshippers, joining their voices in quiet prayer, as they asked for protection from the sea and for a bountiful harvest in their nets.

The line between apprehension and fear is narrow. Discipline and control can keep the one from becoming the other. I had read the current tables for the rapids ahead, columns of numbers that told me the times of tidal highs and lows. From these figures, I calculated the time of slack water. Simple equations, really, but when my life might depend on them, they become more than simple exercises in arithmetic. In a tide-running rapid, they are the equations of survival.

The last foam from the flood tide of Yuculta Rapids was washing down the channel as I approached Gillard and Dent rapids. I waited for the turn to the ebb, and ran through the rapids with trees and shoreline swirling by as the green, moon-powered water carried the boat through.

For another day, I continued to travel the tide-running rivers of Cordero, Chancellor and Wellbore channels to enter Johnstone Strait and a snug anchorage at Tuna Point. The notes from my journal recall that evening:

Anchored Tuna Point on the north shore of Johnstone Strait. At 10 P.M. it is still light. A bright moon hangs in a clear sky flecked with high floating clouds.

Far down the strait, a navigation light begins to blink and across the strait, the mountains of Vancouver Island are in shadows, their ridge lines of snow blue in the lee of the light. On the shore behind me, robins still sing in the trees.

I did nothing during that long evening at Tuna Point except stare at the view, a view I wanted to burn in my mind; I wanted to be able to remember for a long time what it had looked like, from my anchored boat on a summer evening, beneath the mountains looming above Johnstone Strait. Just an evening, looking to remember.

Rain followed me from Tuna Point to Port Neville where I secured the boat to the dock and watched through a windshield streaked with water as the deluge bombed the sea surface into millions of raindrop craters.

Along with the low clouds, a sadness hung over Port Neville. Olaf Hansen, whose father founded Port Neville, was well into his years. He lived there with his wife in the family homestead. Their daughter, Lorna, with her daughter, lived in the only other remaining house. This was the end of the Hansen line at Port Neville. The old log store was closed, its interior a quiet refuge for yellowing papers and records, boxes, bins and shelves no longer stacked with the groceries and supplies of an old outpost community. The barn still stood, and a few chickens pecked around the perimeter of a deer-fenced garden. Slowly the edges of the forest were creeping inward around the fields no longer mown, and bear and cougar wandered just beyond the edge of the clearing.

But young couples have moved in around Port Neville. They are clearing the forests, building homes and scratching out gardens. It is a place enwrapped by the slow curve of time from a long-ago yesterday that can still fulfill people's hopes and desires to create out of forest and sea a home.

From Port Neville, I ran through Johnstone Strait and then turned up through Chatham Channel to enter the Broughton Archipelago, one of the world's most complex clusters of sea islands. Remote when first settled by loggers, fishermen, miners and trappers, the islands today have remained beyond the encroaching reach of development, and the traveler wandering the intricate sea channels that separate the island maze has for his exploration a marine seascape of mountains and forested islands still largely in its natural state, with mink, deer, river otter and bear often seen along the shorelines.

Nature in this sea-island world has but three colors on her palette — the colors of sea, rocks and trees — but with that trio, an infinite variety of shapes, colors and textures are formed by the brush strokes of wind and wave and the damp wash of fog.

On Mound Island, so named because of the large kitchen midden on the shore built up over thousands of years by native people, I watched the advancing front of another rainstorm, a dark, jumbled pile of clouds topped by ragged turrets and pinnacles of black, girded by a brilliant rainbow that arched across the strait. I returned to the boat to let it pass, sat inside with rain drumming on the cabin top and looked out through the doorway to my companion in the storm: a great eagle standing on the high rock of the point, a silhouette in black under a dark sky.

There, I met Mike, a 72-year-old man on the 63rd day of his solo kayak trip from Glacier Bay in Alaska to Seattle. Mike spoke to me about the metronome pace of paddling, of a time of waiting — days of waiting — before he could cross a windy strait. Terribly vulnerable he was, in that tiny kayak, alone on the sea. On and on he paddled, day after day, mile after mile, island after island.

"My mind," he told me, "was filled with what I could see and smell and feel and those thoughts carried me back in time as though I was the first man to travel that sea."

Looking, questioning, wondering, imagining, in the double vision of what is seen and how it is seen — that is the outlook of the explorer and within that perspective lies the ageless thrill of discovery. That is how I traveled those waters, discovering along the way the messages written for everyone in rock and wave and tide and wind and memories.

CHAPTER TEN

A SCHOONER CALLED *HERITAGE*

I HAD REACHED MIDDLE age with two unrequited ambitions still
haunting my mind. One, to own an ocean-going sailboat and,
two, to sail it down the Pacific Coast, through the Panama
Canal and up the Atlantic Coast. To realize both, I sold the little
dory and bought — at a bargain price — the unfinished hull of a
40-foot schooner named *Heritage*.

With the boat sitting there on its building chocks, I visualized
what it would look like completed, with a traditional gaff-headed
rig, sailing across the sea. The wonder of such a possession and my
ignorance and enthusiasm as an amateur boat builder overlooked
the underlying reality, which was that the unfinished hull of 16-
ton, deep-draft wooden boat is thousands of dollars and years of
effort short of a finished boat.

For the first two weeks after I bought the hull, I did nothing but
walk around it, marveling at the anatomy of its massive keel, its
curved sides and its proud, graceful bow. The boat, to me, was like

a wooden jig-saw puzzle except for a huge difference: in a jig-saw puzzle, you find the right pieces and fit them together. I had to first make the pieces and then fit them together.

Along with the hull came a pile of rough-cut timbers and boards. Old and well-seasoned was the lumber that went into that boat. In the rough cutting of timbers to planks, a half-century of wood was discarded as sawdust. The planer then threw out another ten years of growth as it smoothed the boards. Then, as I hand-trimmed a plank, each of my long, curling shavings cut away another year. Finally, I would reach the 50 years of wood I wanted, and a plank would be added to the boat.

Spring to summer, summer to fall, fall to winter and around again, I worked away on that boat, my hands callused and stained with pine tar, but alive, singing of their usefulness. But it was too much. Two years and all the money I had went into that hull and I could see that I was many more years and thousands of dollars away from a finished boat and a voyage. Another man, as ignorant of the demands of building an ocean-going schooner as I had been, bought the boat. Sadly I watched as the great hull was lifted and then chained to the deck of a huge, flatbed trailer, to disappear down the highway and out of my life. What was left behind was the building shed, a large structure of two-by-fours and plywood, and the $20,000 I received for the boat.

Enough lumber in that shed to build a boat, I mused, and out of that musing came the flash of an idea. With the material left in the shed, I could build a small boat, sail it up the Columbia, and then across the continent to the Atlantic, an inland version of the schooner voyage from the Pacific to the Atlantic.

The idea of crossing North America presented me with two questions: Could it be done and could I do it?

The first question I answered by studying a series of Rand McNally maps. They showed that such a passage existed, unbroken except for a short highway portage over the Continental Divide. With a pencil, blue of course, I traced out the route: it went up the Columbia and then up the Snake to the head of navigation at Lewiston, Idaho; then a trailer portage from Lewiston to the old head of navigation on the Missouri River at Fort Benton, Montana;

then down the Missouri to St. Louis, Missouri, up the Mississippi and the Illinois rivers to Lake Michigan; through Lake Michigan and Lake Huron to the Trent-Severn Canal that carried the route to Lake Ontario; down the St. Lawrence, up the Richelieu River to Lake Champlain and from there down the Hudson River to New York City and the Atlantic Coast.

The fascination and challenge of traveling this water route — more than 60 rivers and lakes linked together — supplied the answer to the second question: I wouldn't know if I could cross the continent by boat until I tried.

Out of that shed lumber, I built a little 16-foot, outboard-powered, pram-shaped dory for a total cost of $640.35. The route was there, I had a boat, and there was only one more thing needed: permission to go. Whose permission? *Her* permission, of course, the lady who was my wife, the person I would be leaving behind as I traveled across the continent. She would not give me permission because she declined the authority to bestow it. Instead of permission, she gave me something much better: approval of my intended voyage and an understanding of why I wanted to make it. On my desk, she placed the advice of the old sailor rat in Kenneth Grahame's book, *The Wind in the Willows.* It read:

Take the Adventure, heed the call, now ere the irrevocable moment passes! Tis but a banging of the door behind you, a blithesome step forward, and you are out of the old life and into the new! Then someday, some day long hence, jog home … when the cup has been drained and the play has been played, and sit down by your quiet river with a store of goodly memories for company.

Little did I know what I was about to encounter. It was to be a voyage that, like a living thing, a beast, demanded all my endurance, patience and skill; consumed three boats and four years of my life, and sometimes left me whimpering and crying in its wake. It had its moods of joy, exhilaration and terror as it followed along the twisting, complex water passage of over 5,000 miles that spanned the continent, its moments of anger and madness and sometimes laughter.

It was everything I had wanted. After a thousand miles down the Missouri, a river of windstorm, sandbar and mud banks, I wrote this, my surrender to the voyage and my commitment to its completion:

> Now I am only what the river has made me: a whiskered, mud-caked, sun-burnt man determined to go down this god-damned twisting brown river for another thousand miles or leave my bones along its shores.

On a spring morning, I launched the little boat with the name *Gander* (after my favorite bird, the Canada goose), loaded it with maps and charts, my favorite books and old clothes, the essentials of a gallon of sherry and a pound of pipe tobacco, and motored down to my departure point at the mouth of the Columbia River.

SECTION TWO

VOYAGE ACROSS NORTH AMERICA

CHAPTER ONE

GANDER UP THE COLUMBIA RIVER

I
T WAS SLACK WATER at the time of low tide. My boat lifted and fell with the easy motion of the Pacific swells at the mouth of the Columbia as I waited for the returning tide which would reverse the river's current and carry me upstream and eastward to begin a voyage across North America.

With the first push of the flooding tide, I turned away from the sea in a slow arc and began to run with its stream. Looking back through my camera lens, I could see nothing but the black line of the sea. I snapped a picture, a record of the moment and proof to no one but myself that I had begun the voyage at the Pacific edge of the continent.

The first leg of the voyage would carry me 325 miles up the Columbia and then 138 miles up the Snake River to Lewiston, Idaho, through a series of eight large dams that provide a navigable waterway for tug-and-barge transportation to Lewiston. The first 150 miles of the Columbia is tidal and a part of the river that

62

was very familiar to me: the river of that first rowboat voyage, the summer in the fishing village and my days working aboard the old sternwheeler. I was in a hurry to get above tidewater, to go beyond this area of memories to the upper part of the river I had never explored.

On the first day of the voyage, I traveled 35 miles up the river, and that night wrote the first entry into the log of *Gander:*

In the glimmer of a fading moon, I ended my first day on the river and anchored in a tiny cove. Like a miser counting his gold, I contemplate the treasure of over 5,000 miles yet to go.

The next day, I entered the great gash of the Columbia River Gorge where the river cuts through the high mountains of the Oregon-Washington Cascades. The opening to the gorge is like the entrance to a deep fiord with walls rising steeply from the river to the high summit ridges of the mountains. It is a place of magnificent scenery, carved by forty million years of geological violence and river erosion. Isolated pinnacles and promontories stood above me along the steep basalt terraces that rose, cliff-like, from the river bank.

At Beacon Rock, a free-standing monolith 850 feet high, I left behind me the tidal influence of the Pacific Ocean and started up a river powered by the downhill slant of the continent. I entered the lock at Bonneville Dam, the first of four huge dams that would staircase me up the Columbia. It lifted me 70 feet up and over the dam and then the upstream gate of the lock opened to the view of a different Columbia River. Below the dam, I had traveled past the soft, green shores of a wide, naturally flowing river. Above the dam, I felt imprisoned in a river corridor that was sharp, fixed and linear, the man-made waterline of an impounded lake bordered by highways and railroad tracks.

Wind Mountain was the ominous name of the peak rising before me as I started up through the gorge. It reminded me that the gorge, in addition to scenery, is a place of strong, westerly winds. These winds — as I was soon to experience — can blow for days and, blowing upstream against the river current, can form steep, surf-like waves on the long lakes behind the Columbia River dams.

I passed Wind Mountain in a dead calm and then, only minutes later, the wind started to blow and soon the river was covered with whitecaps that quickly became wind-hammered waves. I made a run for the public dock in Hood River and tied up, wind-bound on a clear, hot summer day.

A couple in a large cruiser tied to the dock were impatient to continue their downriver trip. Around noon, they headed out but in less than an hour they returned. A few miles downstream, they told me, where "the waves were ten feet high," their boat came off a wave and hit the bottom of the trough. All the hatches popped open with the impact, the hinges broke and the hatch lids were blown overboard. The boat's refrigerator was torn from its bulkhead and the toilet flew off its base. The three of us spent the rest of the day safely seated in lawn chairs on the dock.

Dawn, the next morning, was not very encouraging and the gorge below Hood River was filled with wind-streaked clouds. A lightning storm gave a wild touch to the morning. Upriver, a curtain of black clouds was back-lit by the rising sun, its edges pink and orange like the translucent contours of oyster shells.

Gander I.

I tried to get a weather report on my small battery radio but the only program I could hear was a morning bible sermon. I got the word of God from the preacher but nothing about His weather. According to the preacher, it didn't make any difference what the weather was going to do because in his forecast, none of us had long to live anyhow.

Point by point, I worked my way up the river, sometimes hiding out from the wind in the protection of half-submerged trees. Thunder cracked overhead and it began to rain. The rain stilled the wind and in a short period of calm, I made a dash for The Dalles Dam, just upriver from the city of the same name. It had taken me six hours to travel just 21 miles.

The Dalles Dam is a big one, its rim zigzagging two miles from shore to shore. The powerhouse alone is a half-mile long. Its huge single lock is 650 feet long with a lift of 90 feet, the downstream end closed by a towering steel door. I drifted around in front of it, wondering how to open it. Then I spotted a sign that read "Pull the cord to enter." I pulled. Within a few minutes, I heard an electrical buzzing sound and the double gates of the lock swung open to what looked like a huge basement room in the river.

I entered, tied to a floating mooring bitt, and waited like some tiny water bug trapped in a watery pit. The gate closed silently behind me and water began to boil up around me. I peed over the side to add a pint to the millions of gallons of water lifting the boat upwards toward the blue rectangle of sky above me.

The lockmaster greeted me at the top of the lift and said it had taken 430,000,000 gallons of water to lift the boat. "But it's free, compliments of Uncle Sam," he said as he waved me on my way and I putted out on to Lake Celilo.

Dams on a river are something like chapters in a book, each a part of the overall plot but each also introducing a new scene. The scene that greeted me above The Dalles Dam was a river enclosed by high, treeless hills, brown and barren under a hot summer sun. The section behind me, now a closed chapter, was hidden by the lip of the dam and across miles of bright, empty space; the two-mile-high summit of Mount Hood stood cool and aloof above the valley.

That evening I made the mistake of anchoring for the night behind a tiny rock point. It was the only protection I could find along the rock-walled bed of the railroad track. Sometime after midnight, the wind began to blow. My position was less than 15 feet off the stone wall and I realized that if the anchor failed, the boat would be smashed against the rocks in seconds. I packed my wallet and camera in a shoulder bag for a quick get-away if I was forced to leap ashore.

I had a sleepless night with the boat see-sawing wildly around its anchor, one of the worst nights of the entire voyage. An hour before dawn, the wind suddenly dropped and I quickly got under way. Waves were still running, and the boat surfed on the front of every fifth or sixth crest. I was dog-tired and wanted to find a hole somewhere along the shore where I could stop and rest.

I reached the Deschutes River, pulled into the state park just inside the river mouth, and tied the boat to a willow tree in a small cove ringed by soft, green grass. Tiny fish swam in the water that gurgled quietly beneath the boat. I slept through the morning and puttered around all afternoon, restoring order to the boat after the night of storm.

The next morning, just before dawn, I resumed the trip up the Columbia. Headlights from a few cars shone diamond-like as they sped along the highway. Streaks of black basalt, layer upon layer, rose to the crest of the gorge. When the sun lifted above the rim, I traveled in the bottom of a huge canyon of light captured by the river and its sun-yellowed hills. Geese were flying and a fish jumped clear of the quiet water; I had caught the river sleeping, soft and still.

An hour later, I reached the strong current below John Day Dam and the boat's speed was reduced to a crawl. The turbulence of water spilling over the dam made a thick, white foam and I traveled as though crossing a river blanketed by a layer of snow. I reached the lock and pulled the message cord to request passage.

From some place deep inside the dam, a conversation started between ringing bells and squawking klaxon horns. Then the steel guillotine door of the world's highest lock (105 feet) began to rise, lifted by cables hanging from the turrets of its twin guard-towers.

As the gate cleared the river, ribboned sheets of water dropped from its cleaver-shaped lower edge. Open, and hanging above me, it revealed a dead-end tomb of black, wet walls. I hardly had time to moor the boat before some unseen hand touched a button and the huge gate slid noiselessly back into the water. Then, the black water around me began to seethe with up-welling columns of water. Slowly the boat began to rise and I came up from that watery grave to the bright expanse of Lake Umatilla.

> Notes from the Log:
> Since entering the Columbia Gorge above Bonneville Dam, I have been engaged in a contest with the river. I have been knocked about by its winds and battered by its waves. Point by point, mile by mile, I have slowly pushed my way up this river. And now Lake Umatilla: a vast, empty space, one-half a cloudless blue sky framed by golden slopes of rolling, vacant hills and the other half the wide, wide flatness of the 75-mile-long lake.

I remember the day's travel up Lake Umatilla as a delirium of distance. Anticipation was numbed and past was obliterated. I had no other life except that time on the river, no other thoughts except to follow where it led. Mile after mile, hour after hour, I drove the boat along the brown stone wall of a railroad bed. A thin line of driftwood, sun-dried and gray, marked the line between land and water, and my eyes followed hypnotically along that lifeless edge. Where it curved outward, I moved outward; where it curved inward, I turned inward in blind obedience. When I rounded a curve, the river would stretch far ahead of me until it became lost in distance. Then, I would have to spend an hour or so traveling to the end of my view. A train came into sight from upriver, a train whose length I could hide behind the few inches of one finger. When it eventually drew abreast of me, the train of the distant view was nearly a mile long.

The only visible sign of my progress in the vastness of that riverscape was the wake of the boat, a tiny line of water trailing behind that lasted only a moment or so before it disappeared and left no trace of my passage. The flat river, the straight line of the railway and the parallel lines of the shore converged ahead of me to a single point. I traveled toward an optical illusion, a vanishing point at the convergence of water, land and sky, retreating before me in the direction of infinity. Behind me, the river made a long curve to the south and was lost in the blue folds of hills.

Tall power poles marched in rigid formation over the flat Oregon landscape. Their legs and arms were formed of spidery steel and each bore a pyramidal top that looked like a peaked hat. Standing one after another in a straight line across the land, they looked like a parade of clowns, holding between them the draped curves of endless power lines that crossed high above the Columbia in one great span. Bright orange balls, like Christmas ornaments ridiculously out of place, hung from the span. On the soaring towers supporting these wires, strobe lights flashed up and down in precise pulsations of split-second brilliance.

Past the city of Boardman, the railroad turned away from the river and the shoreline was softened by willows along the margins of a beach. Long rows of trees, planted as windbreaks, climbed up the slopes of the Washington shore in straight lines of green and then disappeared over the curve of the hills. I had the river all to myself, miles of river and acres of land without house or car or person in view.

I ran the boat close along the shore, keeping pace with killdeer and small songbirds fluttering and skittering along the edge of the river. Beneath a steep sandbank, I saw where generations of swallows had pecked out thousands of tunneled nests, each slanting upward to give protection to the young swallows inside. Half-asleep, I did not see the black reef that suddenly appeared in front of me. I came instantly awake and veered off to one side, then laughed at myself when the reef lifted off as a flight of geese. Farther on, a flock of gulls took flight from a sandbar as I approached. The near edge of the flock lifted first and set in motion the flight of the other birds, as though the entire flock was one large wing taking to the air. After I passed, the long white line of birds circled and returned to the sandbar, settling down one after the other in the fold of the wing.

I had not seen a person all day and then, rounding a point of land, I nearly collided with the extended fishing poles of two old men seated by the river. I stopped to apologize for my intrusion and then saw they were fast asleep in their wicker chairs, their eyes covered by tipped-down straw hats. Only their old dog, sleeping beneath one of the chairs, lifted a curious head at my approach. He sniffed once, then went back to sleep. I made a wide detour around the point so as not to disturb the lazy, old-fashioned afternoon of two old men and a dog sleeping by the river.

Late that evening, I stopped for the night at Umatilla. The city is just below the high wall of McNary Dam that holds behind it Lake Wallula. "Old Timer," as he called himself, filled my gas cans at the dock. He told me he had spent 50 years on the river and knew all about Lake Wallula.

"When do the winds blow the strongest up there?" I asked him.

"Oh, sometimes in the morning and then sometimes in the afternoon. Never can tell for certain. Sometimes the first half of the day is easy but then you catch hell in the afternoon. Then other times, the first half is awful but the afternoons are fine. I've seen it blow 80 miles an hour up there."

"Was that morning or afternoon?" I asked.

"All day," he replied.

The upper end of the McNary lock swung open for me the next morning and, theatrically, revealed the water-carved history of Lake Wallula in one great view. The lake fills a black-walled channel of high basalt cliffs rising to form the rim of a vast, lonely landscape. Through Wallula Gap, 15,000 years ago, flowed the successive crests of the cataclysmic Bretz Floods that swept down the Columbia River. Author Stewart Holbrook in his book on the Columbia gave this description of the lake and Wallula Gap:

Here on the last notable bend of the Columbia, where it starts its final surge that will take it through the mountains, I saw more of the river than I would have believed possible from one spot. Away to the north it seemed to approach from a horizon infinitely remote; while to the west there was nothing but space and the river for more miles than I cared to guess.

I left the cement-and-steel security of the lock to become the only moving speck in that emptiness of water, land and sky described by Holbrook. I hugged the Oregon shoreline, just below the rock-lined highway edge, and worried about Old Timer's predicted winds. Ahead of me stretched 15 miles of travel without any break, with a highway along the Oregon shore, a railroad track on the Washington shore. For *Gander*, 15 miles would be three hours of exposure, and more than enough time for the wind to start blowing. I knew that once the wind began to blow upriver, there would be no turning back. The slow passing of the picket-like guard posts along the highway reminded me how slowly I was traveling. At 60 miles an hour, they pass in a blur; at five miles an hour, I counted them one by one.

For two hours the air remained calm as I headed up the river. Then, a gentle breeze began to play at the back of my neck. Minutes later, whitecaps formed across the river and I knew that soon the river would be too dangerous for the little *Gander*. I could neither hide from the wind nor outrun it, but I knew that I had to do something.

Ahead of me, the river made a long curve to the northeast. In the lee of that curve, I thought, the wind would be less. But getting to the other shore meant crossing the river which, at mid-channel, was already a washboard of wind-against-current waves. For almost too long I clung to the false security of the rock-walled Oregon shore. Then I summoned up all my courage and turned the boat at right angles to the wind for a dash across the river. Whitecaps broke around the boat and seethed down the backsides of the waves in fingers of foam. The boat rolled in wave troughs, dishes and pans fell from their cupboards and crashed to the floor. I steered with one hand around the tiller, the other clinging to a handrail so that I could remain standing. The shore behind me seemed to cling to my stern, the one in front of me appeared no closer. Not a solitary eye was witness to my wild ride across the river, not even a bird.

Finally, I closed with the Washington shore and found a narrow ribbon of calmer water paralleling the land. It carried me safely through Wallula Gap and around the bend where the Columbia headed north toward Canada. It was windless and warm around that corner and I anchored in a small cove. Just below me, wind and waves streamed through the gap, the last passage of my Columbia River voyage. A few miles upstream lay the mouth of my next river, the Snake.

Chapter Two

GANDER UP THE SNAKE RIVER

ONE ARE THE OLD colorful names for the rapids of the Snake River: Washboard, Deadman Creek, Dry Gulch, Devil's Bend. Buried now are those old obstacles to river travel, beneath the impounded waters behind the four dams that provide a slack-water passage all the way to Lewiston. I regretted not at all their disappearance. The prospect of slack water ahead appealed to me after the bouncing I had endured on the Columbia. But each river has its price that one must pay for traveling it. On the Snake, that would be heat, bake-oven heat that would fry me in the narrow and windless river canyon.

I came up to Ice Harbor Dam, the first one on the Snake, feeling that after the big locks on the Columbia, the smaller one at Ice Harbor would be easy. Nothing to it, I thought as I tied up in the lock and waited for the lock-master to take me through.

Tied up and waited …

A head leaned over the edge of the lock above me.

"Hey, you," came the voice. "If you untie your boat from the bottom of the ladder, I'll lock you up."

In disbelief, I looked at my mooring line. My God, he was right. I had tied the boat to the bottom rung of a fixed steel ladder. Had the lock-master not noticed and released water into the lock, the boat would have been pinned to the bottom of the lock beneath a hundred feet of water. Terribly embarrassed, I apologized when I floated up to him, cleared the lock and hurried toward anonymity behind the first bend in the river.

Low hills formed a backdrop to the river above Ice Harbor Dam. On the flat land between river and hills, irrigated islands of green made large circles on the land, the circumferences of the circles defined by long sprinkler pipes rotating above the ground on spindly legs. I saw two dust storms whirl along the top of some unnamed ridge, dancers that twirled in unison, became one, and disappeared down the other side.

It was only mid-morning but already hot. Very hot. I sloshed my shirt overboard, pulled it dripping wet from the river, and plastered it around my shoulders. I cringed at the first touch of cold, wet cloth on my hot skin, then snuggled into its fresh coolness. I stopped for lunch in a small inlet, shut off the engine and listened to the river's stillness. It was a stillness filled with bird songs and singing bugs. I went swimming and, while in the water, I washed down the boat. A few grains of sand had accumulated in a corner of the cockpit, carried aboard by my feet after a walk along some island beach on the lower Columbia. I sponged them out and watched them settle through the water to the river bottom. Grains of sand that perhaps 10,000 years ago had washed down the Snake to the Columbia, a journey they would now begin again.

Under way again, I became mesmerized by the heat and the steady drone of the engine and the unbroken solitude of the vacant and empty shores. There was no relief, only more river and more heat. I drew inward, as though to expose less of me to the sun. My eyes bored into the green coolness of the river and as I looked closer and closer into nothing but river passing beneath me, I discovered more and more things to see in the tight circle of my vision. I watched with fascination the line of bubbles that formed and broke along the side of the boat as it pushed a green furrow through the flat river. I saw grasshoppers swimming and bits of dandelion fluff that floated in the air under tiny umbrellas and skimmed along the sun-glazed skin of the river. Carp, wavering in the shadows under tufts of water grass, swam away with a great splashing and flopping of their tails as I overran their cool retreat.

Notes from the Log:
Mid-afternoon so hot I put up my rain umbrella to make some shade. I would present a bizarre picture out here on the river if anyone were to see me: odd-shaped boat traveling up a heat-scorched river with a man standing at the tiller under a rain umbrella smoking a pipe and sipping warm gin from a coffee cup. I rather like the picture and am glad I am the man in it. It's all reminiscent of mad dogs and Englishmen braving it out in the midday sun.

I went through a checklist of things to do as I approached Lower Monumental Dam so that I would not repeat the fiasco of Ice Harbor Dam. Fenders were made ready; reading glasses on so that I could read the fine print on the instruction board; gin bottle and pipe out of the way; mooring lines ready to be tied to something that would float instead of to the bottom of a ladder. My worry was that the lock-master at Ice Harbor Dam might have called ahead to warn the lock-master at Lower Monumental to be on the lookout for a crazy fool in a small blue boat. If so, the attendant at Lower Monumental politely said nothing as he waved me on up the river.

Above the dam, the Snake changed character. Here, the land seemed to resent the passage of the river and pressed its domain to the very edge of the water where it ended in broken basalt toes that formed the river bank. Only two trees were in sight in the four-mile section of river opening to my view as I came out of the lock. Nothing else was green in that brown, scarred land of broken rock terraces rising high above the Snake. In places, the river had cut away the cliffs to create overhanging lips. Under these overhangs, swallows had built thousands of nests that hung from the rock like mud-colored fruit. Black ravens leaped ahead of me from point to point along the ridge line of the high cliffs. At twilight, after 13 hours on the river, I turned in through a huge drainpipe that led me to Ayers Boat Basin. For my first day on the Snake, I had traveled 50 miles along its heated coils.

It was already hot when I pulled out of the boat basin the next day at dawn to begin another scorching day. It was the birth-morning for millions of tiny spiders drifting across the windless river on long silver threads that trailed behind them. The mast and windshield of the boat were soon wrapped in a shimmering gauze of silken pennants that waved gently in the breeze made by the boat's forward motion.

Little Goose Dam was the seventh in my staircase voyage upriver. I was approaching the end of the voyage on the Snake as a dry, stiff, stringy and parched traveler. Under that torrid August sun, through the heat and distance of the river, all I could do was endure one hour, one mile at a time. Memory was the curve of the river behind me, the future was the curve ahead as I traveled on with a wet towel wrapped around my head like an Arab's burnoose. The shoreline ahead wavered in heat and the line between water and shore merged in the molten light. No trees, no shade anywhere. The thermometer on the cabin wall had reached the limit of its gauge — 120 degrees.

I saw thousands of bugs jumping up and down on a thin line of beach below a high, sandy cliff. Closer, I saw they were tiny grasshoppers that had hatched on the beach below the cliff and were frantically trying to escape from their prison of river and sand. Springing on hinged legs, they leaped again and again into the air, clung for a second to the dry, crumbling sand, then fell back to the beach to die where they had come into the world. Farther along, a cow lay dead on the same beach. It had fallen from the sand cliff, probably in trying to get to the river for a drink. Unable to escape, it had died like the grasshoppers.

Finally, the sun dropped below the rim of the canyon and I traveled on the shaded edge of the river beneath the cliffs. Geese appeared and flew low over the water and swallows began to dart back and forth on their evening quest for insects. Cool air dropped through gullies of eroded rock to fall like a refreshing waterfall from the sky.

I anchored for the night in a small cove surrounded by a tight jungle of dry, bristly brush. The cove was filled with the zinging hum of millions of unseen bugs hiding in the brown, lifeless grass. It was too hot to sleep so I placed bug screens on the windows and crawled into the bunk to read. I had read only a few pages when I became conscious of something pressing in on the screens, something close and stifling. Countless tiny bugs were hurling their bodies against the screen to get at my reading light. The corners of the window were filled with their crawling bodies and the screen was covered with writhing wings, legs and bodies. To save the lives of thousands of insects, I turned out the light and sat through the evening in a darkened cabin.

The next day — my last on the Snake — I was under way before dawn. Heat lightning flashed somewhere off to the south and the sky was fuzzed with clouds. The air over the river was still warm, a leftover bowl of yesterday's heat. Ladybugs by the hundreds crawled along the deck and cabin top of the boat. Slowly they left, their tiny wings beating at invisible speed as they launched themselves for the long flight across the wide river.

The lights of Lower Granite Dam twinkled ahead in the early light like a line of birthday candles across the river. It was the last of the eight dams on my western river voyage. After I was locked through to the lake behind the dam, I was 783 feet above the level of the Pacific Ocean where I had started.

I smelled Lewiston's pulp mills long before I reached the city. I found a dock, moored the boat, and walked through the streets on a deserted Sunday morning. Music blaring out from a mainstreet store played to empty sidewalks. I waited outside a restaurant for it to open, had breakfast, and returned to the boat. Lewiston was not a destination for me; it was only the turn-around point on the rivers that had taken me there. To the east, over the Continental Divide, was another river: the Missouri. My thoughts were on that river, another summer, and another voyage, as I headed the *Gander* downstream for the return voyage to Portland. Like the river itself, I was going home to begin again.

Chapter Three

SHIPWRECKED IN MONTANA

AFTER I RETURNED TO Portland, I studied the waterways I had yet to travel and decided I needed a larger boat for the 4,000-mile voyage still ahead. The postman bought the little *Gander* and I built a type of boat known as a "St. Pierre dory." It had originally been developed by the French government as a low-cost fishing boat for the sea fisheries around the French-owned islands of St. Pierre and Miquelon in the Gulf of St. Lawrence.

Naval architect John Gardner adapted the original lines of the boat to a pleasure craft and *Gander II* was built from those plans. It had a length of 24 feet, a beam of eight feet and a draft of 18 inches. The new boat had a large, comfortable cabin, a wood-stove, two bunks, a galley area and a 16-horsepower inboard engine. It took me a winter, a spring and part of the next summer to build it. By late summer, the boat was finished and my friend Jim Gillis agreed to use his truck to haul it from Portland over the Continental Divide to Fort Benton, Montana, on the upper Missouri, and then spend a few weeks traveling down the river with me.

We crossed the Continental Divide through McDonald Pass, the boat on its trailer at the 6,250-foot high pass looking like a huge, dry-land fish. We entered eastern Montana on the other side of the divide and the country looked terribly dry as we drove north from Great Falls to Fort Benton.

"Driest in years," the Bureau of Land Management agent at Fort Benton told us. "Last week," he said, "I ran aground in the river in a canoe."

He advised us to begin the voyage 150 miles downstream at James Kipp Park. Regretfully, because we would miss running the wild, upper part of the Missouri, we accepted his advice and drove down to the park. There, to our dismay, we saw that the lower end of the launching ramp — normally in the water — was six feet above the level of the river.

I proposed that we back the boat and trailer to the end of the ramp, coat both the bottom of the boat and the trailer bed with grease, give the boat a big push and hope it would land in the river.

Gander II.

Two fishermen standing by helped give the boat a big shove. It started sliding, gained momentum, and shot out into the river with me tied to it by the bow-rope I held in my hand. Boat and I, in a hilarious launch, were both floating in the Missouri.

In the afternoon, with all in order, we started down the river. Jim stood on the bow with a long bamboo pole he used to sound the water. We bumped a few times on mud banks but most of the time found deep water running in the main channel. That night we went to sleep with coyotes singing to a full moon and I drifted off, content with the thought that the voyage ahead was mostly downhill to the Atlantic. It was the last happy night aboard *Gander II*.

We were under way again the next morning as soon as it was light. Slowly, we traveled down the river through the morning and afternoon, following one gentle curve and then another as the river carried us along. We grounded a few times but all it took to get us back in the main channel was a push with Jim's pole. Around three in the afternoon, the river widened and the current no longer ran with any significant force. We had arrived at the upper end of Fort Peck Lake which lies in the nearly roadless, million-acre Charles M. Russell National Wildlife Refuge.

Looking back, I noted that the propeller wash was churning up a long trail of mud. I slowed the engine to give Jim time to probe for deeper water. Carefully, he measured the depth along both sides of the boat. Nowhere was it deeper than a foot or so. We had skidded aground and were stuck in 12 inches of water with a 3,000-pound boat drawing 18 inches. Together, Jim and I pushed on poles and rocked the boat from side to side but it would not budge. We were not too alarmed. Tomorrow, we assumed, we would just tow the boat to deeper water.

The next morning I jumped overboard with a towing rope and immediately sank to my crotch in thick, squishy mud. With each step, I sank deeper and I had the terrible thought that we had grounded in quicksand. (Later we were told that the river bottom in that area is composed of a fine sediment called "diatomaceous earth," just slightly more stable than quicksand.)

"Jim, we can't walk in that stuff," I said as I climbed back aboard. "We'll have to somehow carry out an anchor, bury it and then pull the boat to it."

I tied a life jacket around me and then, with a 20-pound anchor in one hand and 160 feet of rope trailing behind, I half crawled and half "mud swam" to the end of the rope. Then I dug a shallow hole with my hands for the anchor and pushed it deeper into the mud by stomping on it with my feet. I pulled myself back to the dory on the anchor line and crawled aboard, skin scratched and gritty with mud from head to foot.

Jim then hauled on the anchor line while I tried to run the boat ahead under full throttle. It would not budge. We got out a shovel and tried to clear the mud under the keel, but each little trough we dug was quickly filled again by the soupy consistency of the river bottom. We put out another anchor, this one tied to a block and tackle, to give additional pulling power. Nothing we did moved the boat more than a few feet and we went to bed too tired to clean off the gobs and patches of mud that had accumulated from bow to stern.

All during the next day, we dug with our hands and the shovel trying to carve out a channel ahead of the boat. We pushed on the pole, pulled on the anchor line and I almost burned up the engine running it at full speed, hoping the propeller wash would dig a channel. We were able to move *Gander II* only a few feet. It was exhausting work and our skin, because of the scouring action of the grit we worked in, looked as though it had been sandpapered. Late in the day, I tied all the anchor ropes together to make one line almost 300 feet long. Our hope was that with a longer line, we might be able to pull harder on the anchor with a stronger, more sustained effort. I started out with the anchor and at the end of 30 minutes of mud-crawling I stopped to rest and discovered that I had left the rope on the boat. I had hauled out only the anchor and its chain.

I returned to the boat completely done in. Jim then made the crawl out with rope, anchor and chain, buried the anchor, and pulled himself back to the boat. We knew it would be our last effort because both of us were totally exhausted. The last try failed; we could do no more.

Jim voiced the unmentionable; we would have to abandon the boat. In all our efforts to free it, I had never thought of that awful possibility: a new boat, barely a hundred miles along on its maiden voyage, now to be abandoned. That evening I went to sleep knowing it would be my last night aboard *Gander II*. I looked at the little woodstove, the comfortable bunks, the shelves of books and dishes, the hanging pots and pans, all the things that make up the wonderful and sheltered interior security of a boat. I imagined it sinking slowly in the river mud and the slow rise and spread of the muck as it filled the inside of the cabin and then buried the boat. My boat, a grave of hopes, dreams and ambitions, gone down and lost in the bottomless mud of the Missouri River.

The next morning we cleaned the boat inside and out, washed all the dishes and returned everything — charts, tools, books and clothing — to its proper place so that *Gander II* would go to its grave in full cruising neatness and order. We assumed that once ashore, we would have to walk some distance to reach a road or a farmhouse, so we took very little, just cameras, wallets, two sleeping bags, a half case of beans and a bottle of cognac. All of this fitted into two canvas bags that we carried over our shoulders as we waded ashore.

We were in no danger. The weather was warm. We had a reasonable amount of food and a river to drink. The problem was where to go and in which direction? We climbed a bluff above the river to get a view. Nothing: no house, no road, no barn, no telephone wires, just empty brush land for as far as we could see. There was what appeared to be a faint track across a field but we did not know where it came from or where it led. Instead of striking out for nowhere, we decided that the sensible thing to do was to stay where we were for a while.

I spent most of the afternoon up on that bluff, looking out over the river and at the tiny speck in the distance that was my abandoned boat.

"Okay, old man," I thought to myself, "you got this far and you lost your boat. You've had your adventure and now it's time to go home and garden with Her."

It was lonely up there on the bluff with the mile-wide Missouri below me — very lonely — and I wanted to turn away from the river, from the memory of the awful days of mud-swimming, and just go home. Then I recalled what we had seen during our few days on the Missouri: the river bank sliding by as the river flowed on to the next curve and the curve after that; pelicans crossing the wide line of the river, looking, in the refracted light of the water, like small white ponies meadowing on the river; the geese that flew up before us with their honking cries of alarm as we traveled along the banks of the river wilderness. And I thought, "No, it's not time to quit this voyage. Two boats have taken me this far. With a third boat I could continue on. Go down the Missouri and then across the continent."

With these thoughts, *Gander III* was conceived and I sketched its lines in the dust with a stick. It would be a flat-bottomed, barge-type boat. A shallow-draft boat that could skim across shallow water, follow me wherever I could wade. A boat so simple to build that I could be back on the Missouri the following spring.

But first, Jim and I had to get home.

Rex and Betty Kaufman had set out that morning from their home in Malta, Montana, to visit their friends, Ralph and Ada Young. The Youngs were living in a house trailer for the summer while they strung fences across ranchlands. After lunch, the two couples went for a drive and at a dirt intersection Betty said, "Rex, let's see what's at the end of that road." At the end of the road they found Jim and me, two mud-caked, whiskered derelicts cast up from the river. We explained our situation and pointed to the boat as proof of our story.

"Don't need to prove it," said Rex. "You look like a couple of guys in trouble and in Montana no questions are asked when a fellow is in trouble."

The Kaufmans drove us to Malta (it would have been a 40-mile walk for Jim and me) and insisted we stay at their home. After a shower and dinner, we told them the full story of our misadventure. Rex immediately got on the phone and started calling people he thought might be able to help.

Over the next few days, calls came in from various agencies and individuals offering floats, rescue boats, tractors and man-power. Men dropped by the house to discuss possible rescue operations.

Our problem was that any boat sent to rescue *Gander II* would also become stuck in the mud. Even if the boat were pulled ashore, there was no way it could be lifted up and over the high bluffs along the river edge. The governor of Montana called in to say he was requesting an air force helicopter lift. The air force turned down the request because no lives were in danger and because the air force could not, by law, engage in the salvage business.

One by one, all the rescue schemes were discussed and discarded. I sat there, disappointed that nothing could be done but amazed that so many were trying so hard to do so much for a couple of strangers who had been dumb enough to come down the Missouri in a boat designed for ocean fishing.

In a tavern where Jim and I ordered a beer, the barman recognized us.

"You're the guys that got stuck in the river, aren't you. Beer here is free as long as you're in town."

The town had offered all it had to give. Rex drove us back to Jim's truck and trailer in Montana. For Rex, it was a 600-mile round trip, but he refused to let us even fill the gas tank for him. As we left him, the words of an unknown Arab poet came to my mind:

> How often, when the country is barren and dry,
> The people are more generous than nature.
> Not scorning their fellow man
> But giving, as naturally as the wind blows.

There was a sequel to the story of our Montana shipwreck. My insurance company put the boat up for sale "as is and where is." A fellow from Fort Peck, Montana, bought it. He had a jet boat and he used it to cut a channel deep enough for *Gander II* to be towed through. He then started out to tow it back to Fort Peck. On the way, a sudden storm came up and the jet boat sank. The fellow climbed aboard *Gander II* and made it back to Fort Peck.

We returned home from Montana on a Saturday. By the following Tuesday, I was at work on *Gander III*. It took me just seven weeks to build that boat — the flat-bottomed, barge-type boat I had designed in the dust of the Missouri River bluff — 24 feet long, six feet wide with a draft of less than four inches. And then I waited, waited for the winter snows to fall and for the spring to melt the snow and for the Missouri to rise. With that rise, I would be ready. Ready to return to the Missouri.

CHAPTER FOUR

DOWN THE MISSOURI RIVER

T HE MISSOURI RIVER RUNS for over 2,000 miles through seven states (Montana, North Dakota, South Dakota, Iowa, Nebraska, Kansas and Missouri), ripping and chewing at the land to earn its nickname, the "Big Muddy." Fort Benton, the old head of steamboat navigation on the Missouri was, in its time, the farthest inland port in the world, 3,575 miles up the Mississippi and the Missouri from the Gulf of Mexico. Commercial navigation today ends at Sioux City, Iowa, 734 miles up the Missouri from the confluence at St. Louis. Above there, six huge dams hold the river in lakes that cover millions of acres of old prairie lands, lakes whose far shores often fall below the horizon.

Boone Caudill, the violent mountain man in A.B. Guthrie's book *The Big Sky*, understood the dimensions and the sweep of the Missouri.

The river went on, to the Mandans, to the Minitari, to the Knife River, to the Little Missouri, the brown never-ending

river, idling and tearing and twisting and gouging, the river that
ran full of silt and drift and rotting buffalo, leading up from the
deep woods and closed hills and the scrub grass of the down
country to country that kept getting freer and bigger until
sometimes, looking out over it from a rise, Boone felt he was
everywhere on it, like the air or the light.

"God damn, Jim" [says Boone to his companion].

"What?"

"This here. Everything."

"Everything" was what my journey down the Missouri was for
me; everything a voyage, an adventure and a challenge could be.
Impatiently, I waited through that winter after building *Gander III*
for a return to the Missouri, to go down that "brown never-ending
river." Jim Gillis also felt the Missouri's challenge and he returned
to the river with me the following spring, hauling the new boat
behind his truck.

We crossed the Continental Divide through Rogers Pass and
then dropped down out of the mountains into the early spring of
eastern Montana. The hills were golden with acres of dandelions
and the streams filled with water running eastward to join the
Missouri. By mid-afternoon of the second day of driving, we were
back in Fort Benton and this time we saw a river running full and
deep past the town.

The next morning, we started down the river and immediately
the Missouri took charge of the boat with its slow-moving current.
The drifting pace of the boat in the brown river was so peaceful
that we ignored the engine, rigged bow and stern steering oars, and
traveled in silence. All the planning, the despair of the lost boat, the
work of building a replacement, all of that was in the past. We were
back on the Missouri, drifting with its currents to wherever and
whatever they might carry us.

Before us lay a trip of 300 miles through one of the loneliest
regions of the United States to the town of Fort Peck, Montana.
"Hell with the fires out" was how General Alfred Sully described
the area when he passed through it in 1864. It has changed very
little since then. The river passes through the Missouri Breaks, the

Gander III, *on a trial run before the trip.*

name given to the steep and eroded bluffs left by the cutting action of the river. The first 150 miles of the Missouri below Fort Benton runs through a spectacularly scenic section of Montana, a tumbled, serene and overwhelming landscape of naked ridges, domes, buttes and bare hills.

We stopped for the night 26 miles below Fort Benton and were treated to an after-dinner symphony of Montana weather, a roaring, pelting rainstorm of crackling lightning and shattering thunder as a conclusion to our first day on the river.

Notes from the Log:
Awake to a cool morning and get under way by just floating away from our island camp to begin a day of river drifting. Wind bounces off the hills, now blowing upstream, now down, and we pivot and twirl in midstream at the caprice of wind and current. My fishing bobber follows obediently behind the boat at the end of its line, catching nothing but long green strands of grass. We hear only the sound of the river, the cooing of doves in the trees and the honking of geese that fly up before us. A late afternoon storm catches us on the river. We rig a rain tarp over the cockpit

and drift along, smoking our pipes as we look out at wet, gray cliffs slipping by across a river dimpled by raindrops. We anchor at Wolf Island for a second night of rain, wind, lightning and thunder. At midnight, I thrash ashore through the storm, through mud and scrub brush, to set out a second tie-line to hold the boat in the shrieking wind.

The next day, we entered the river section called "White Cliffs," a geological fantasy of weathered sandstone. The European traveler, Alexander Philip Maximilian, who went up the Missouri in 1832, saw in these formations "pulpits, organs with their pipes, old ruins, fortresses, castles and churches with painted towers." John Neihardt, who traveled down the Missouri by canoe in 1908, saw "soaring mosques and mystic domes ... all like the visible dream of a master architect gone mad."

The sun came out as Jim and I passed beneath such famous formations as Castle Rock, Citadel Rock and Cathedral Rock, looking today exactly as those early river travelers described them. Then, adding wonders to wonders, Jim found on the shore the fossilized jawbone of some ancient, toothy sea monster as long as his arm, evidence of the sea that covered the area millions of years ago. He also found a petrified chambered nautilus that would have filled a washtub.

On the fourth day, we passed James Kipp Park where *Gander II* had been launched to begin its ill-fated voyage. High water had completely changed the river and our entry into Fort Peck Lake was through a maze of channels wandering through a forest of drowned, black trees.

It was late afternoon when we reached the cloud-darkened waters of the open lake. Long lines of pelicans skimmed over its charcoal surface and high in the sky, other bands circled in the air like specks of white confetti carried aloft by the wind. We were full of apprehension as we approached the shallow area where the boat had been lost, a lonely place of awful memories that we were entering on the dark edge of a rising storm.

Jim went forward to stand on the bow. I slowed the engine and we crept ahead. My toes seemed to almost curl under my feet as they waited to feel the slithering of a second grounding. *Gander III* was designed and built to get through this one shallow stretch of the river. Again — out of the nightmares that had haunted me — there was that tell-tale streak of muddy water behind the boat, churned up by the engine.

"Shallow water!" I hollered to Jim.

Immediately, we both jumped overboard into the well-remembered crotch-deep mud. He towed and I pushed as both of us struggled through that shallow, wide, dark and windswept lake that hissed and seethed under driving rain. Then, it was all over; we had skidded over the bottom and reached waist-deep water. We climbed aboard, downed a glass of rum, and continued on down the river.

It took us two days to cover the remaining 100 miles to the town of Fort Peck. The weather had cleared and we followed close along the south shore of the lake. It was a landscape even larger than what I had encountered on the Columbia, an immense, open space of hills, bluffs and eroded coulees, dry, nearly treeless and beautiful in its stark, lean wildness. I had the impression that we were seeing the land as it existed when it was the domain of the Indian nations, bare yet bountiful with life. We were astounded by the number of antelope we saw gathered in huge herds along the shore. We could see them miles ahead, yellow-brown streaks of color that would break into hundreds of separate shapes as the animals fled ahead of the boat. The herds would run along the beach until they encountered a ridge line leading to the sheltering hills above the lake. One by one, they would climb the ridge and prance along its summit in an orderly, single file and then disappear behind its crest. We counted over 300 antelope in many of these herds.

We arrived at Fort Peck Dam after six days on the river. During that time, we had not seen another boat or person on the river or along its shores.

CHAPTER FIVE

LAKES OF THE RIVER

A T FORT PECK, JIM had to return home and I was faced with the job of getting the boat over the first dam (none of the Missouri River dams had locks). I had constructed a set of detachable wheels that were supposed to convert the boat into its own trailer so it could be hauled around the Missouri dams. I attached the wheels to the boat; the marina manager hooked his truck to the boat and started to pull it up the ramp. As soon as the boat became a trailer, the wheel assembly collapsed. All the spectators had a good laugh and the marina manager used his own truck and trailer to get me over that first dam. He asked $15 for the tow; I countered with $50, and headed on down the river.

Jim was gone and I was alone, alone on the river and also alone in the sense that no one knew where I was as the current carried me down the Missouri, around the bend and out of sight of Fort Peck. In a way, it was as though the voyage was beginning again — a long one — and a new perspective of time and distance was needed. The 450 miles up the Columbia and Snake rivers had seemed, at the time, like a long voyage. Now, I had to think of the nearly 1,800 miles ahead of me on the Missouri, a distance longer than an Atlantic Ocean crossing between Brazil and Africa. Yet that long journey was something I anticipated. It would be a test, a test in which I would have to discipline myself to the mile-by-mile dimensions of the time and place in which I existed, a discipline to "be where I was" on the river and not in some anticipated future of time and place. For now, that time and place was somewhere in eastern Montana on a now swift-flowing river that required my full attention to navigate.

The river was a continuous series of wide S-curves, one after the other. As it curved, separate channels formed — some shallow, some blind leads — but only one main channel. Sometimes I picked the right channel and the boat would sweep around the wide outside turn of the curve. Many times I guessed wrong; then I had to get out and tow the boat across a sandbar.

As the river made its curves, it undercut trees that toppled into the water. Many of these trees, called "sweepers," remained fixed to the shore by their roots, and their trunks projected out into the river to form dams that collected and held huge masses of drift. The sweepers I could see and avoid but not the nearly invisible trees whose roots had become snagged on the bottom. The tops of these trees had been sheared off when the river ice began to move, and now their spear-pointed tops lurked just below the level of the spring high waters.

Other trees had been caught on the bottom with their branches still intact. The current, pushing against these limbed trees, forced them to the bottom but when the tension became too great, they would spring upwards, and suddenly — where nothing had been — a tree would thrash up in front of me, huge and black. I traveled with the awful anticipation of hearing and feeling one of these hidden monsters suddenly coming up beneath the boat to either tip it over or pierce its bottom. A hastily jotted log note recorded my difficulties:

> Go too far to one side of the channel and I hazard hitting the hidden trees. Go too far to the other side and I run aground.

Run too slow and the strong, upriver wind blows me off course.
Run too fast and I hazard being sunk by an unseen log.

The next day, running down from Wolf Point, Montana, to
the confluence of the Yellowstone and the Missouri, I concentrated on trying to understand the way of the river and to find
logic and order in what appeared to be a chaotic confusion of
mud banks, shallows, channels and snags. On the Columbia and
the Snake, channel buoys showed me the way but on the upper
Missouri there were no such aids and I had to learn how to
"read" the river.

I noticed that wading pelicans favored the downriver tips of
hidden spits; ergo, stay away from wading pelicans. I saw that the
river turned like a huge half-wheel around the point of a curve;
that the wheel then collapsed and out of it flowed numerous
streams that reassembled in one channel as the river gathered itself
to go around the next curve. The course to follow, I saw, was not
just down the river but back and forth across the river from one
shore to the other in the serpentine sweep of the main channel. I
learned to pause at the top of each curve, slow the engine, ask
aloud, "River, which way do you go?" and then follow my decision,
hoping that no hidden tree snags lay in my path.

It required total, exhausting concentration: eyes looking ahead to
spot the channel and then into the water immediately in front of
the boat looking for the tell-tale "V" of slithering water that would
mark the location of an underwater tree top. I lost all sense of
location because I could not remember how many bridges I had
passed under. One bridge meant I had not gone very far; two
bridges would have told me I had traveled quite a distance. The
problem was only marginally interesting. Wherever I was, I was
simply following the river.

Notes from the Log:
Passed the mouth of the Yellowstone River. Bare feet badly
sunburned and swollen from standing all day. Three stout gin
and bitters add to the almost mystical detachment of my mood.
Boat and I seem a part of the river, we three flowing as one.

Two men in two canoes appeared below a bend, the first people I had seen on the river in almost 400 miles of travel. They came alongside and introduced themselves as Daniel and Robert. Both were in their mid-20s. They had started out on separate trips down the Missouri but had teamed up to make the trip together after a chance meeting above Great Falls. I offered them a ride, they accepted, and with the two canoes towed astern, we traveled down the river together. Never had I encountered two such dissimilar traveling companions.

Daniel, with his scraggly beard, looked like a riverman-trapper of the last century. He wore a pointed black hat that shaded a sun- and wind-burnt face. His pant legs were torn off just below his knees, his shirt sleeves just below the elbows, and small fur pieces, tails and feathers, adorned what was left of his ragged clothing. His canoe was piled high fore and aft with axes, shovels, a rifle, rolls of canvas, iron pots and packsacks, all lashed together with knotted and frazzled ropes.

Robert, on the other hand, looked as though he were heading to a tennis match. His eyes were shaded by a stiff, white visor that ringed a head of neatly trimmed hair. His white T-shirt was tucked into a pair of tight-fitting white shorts and he wore white tennis shoes. Specially made packs and bags fitted together in his canoe in tidy bundles and were tied together with brightly colored plastic ropes.

Daniel was equipped with the make-do and the second-hand. Robert's equipment looked as if it had just come from the L.L.Bean store. When we camped that night, Daniel hung a dirty and torn tarp from a rope tied to a tree, threw his packs under it and called it home. Robert very carefully sought out a high place on the beach where he erected a light, airy tent supported by slender arches of aluminum rods. Daniel built a fire, got out his blackened pots and pans, and cooked up a dinner of bread and beans. Robert had little packs of dried and canned food he prepared over a small propane camp stove.

Daniel seemed impervious to the mosquitoes humming around his head. Robert sprayed the grass around his tent and himself with a little pressure can of scented repellent. After dinner, Daniel sharpened his knife and his axe, then lay back against his pack to drink a cup of wicked, black coffee. Robert went down to the river edge where he washed his clothes in a little plastic bucket and hung them on a line with tiny clothes pins.

Whatever their differences, they were competent travelers and both had projected long, long journeys by paddle. Daniel had already camped through the freezing winter temperatures of Montana and Robert had started his voyage on the headwaters of the Missouri in snow. Their destination, when I dropped them near Williston, North Dakota, was New Orleans, far down the Missouri and Mississippi rivers.

Below Williston, I entered the strange, flooded forest lying at the head of 178-mile-long Lake Sakakawea. The lake was created by the construction of Garrison Dam and is one of the largest man-made lakes in the world. It floods an area of 368,000 acres enclosed by a shoreline of 1,600 miles.

My Corps of Engineers charts of the lake showed parallel lines that defined where the old river channel had been before the river was dammed. Outside the margins of these lines were areas marked "Hazard Area, Submerged Trees." I was uncertain about the locations of these because the wide lake was bordered by a shoreline without significant marks or features, so I took a middle course down the lake and promptly got lost in a flooded forest. I kept the sun in front of me for direction and slowly traveled through fields of waving tulle grass and avenues of stiff, dead, naked trees 20 to 30 feet high. Many of the leads I followed ended in impassable thickets of bleak, lifeless branches. Each dead end required a turn around and a search for another opening through the forest.

My gas tanks were low on fuel and the awful thought occurred to me that if I ran out of gas while chasing one blind lead after another, I could become marooned in the forest. I was miles from either shore. The water was too cold for swimming and too deep for wading. No one would ever come to my rescue. Becoming lost in that weird, drowned forest hardly seemed a good excuse for losing a second boat on the Missouri, but lost I was and growing desperate as the fuel gauge hovered at zero. Finally I broke through and made it to the marina at Lewis and Clark State Park. I arrived with the engine working on little more than gas fumes.

Traveling down Lake Sakakawea, the abstract figure of its 1,600-mile shoreline became a geographic reality, one I had to endure. I became terribly bored. There was nothing special to see, nothing to concentrate on and no change in the passing scenery. No one hill differed from another and there was no shoreside house or farm to evoke mild curiosity about the people who lived by this huge lake. Just going five, ten miles in a straight line to a point that had been visible for an hour. I would reach it, change course slightly, and head for the next distant point.

Two days and 90 miles later, I rounded a headland called Independence Point and looked north into the emptiness of Van Hook Arm. It was only a side arm of the main lake but even so, its entrance was five miles wide and the far end of the arm dropped below my horizon. I rounded another point and there, stretching ahead of me in one immense view to the east, was the 50 miles of the next day's travel. All tomorrow, I thought, I will be seeing what I can see today.

"Private" read the sign on the little lakeshore dock. I asked the man standing next to it if I could tie up for the night.

"Tie up, wash up, and then come up to the house for dinner," he replied.

I needed no second invitation and an hour later I was seated on the deck of his house eating fresh fish, barbecued ribs and steak, and drinking cold beer with the first North Dakota families I had ever met. One of my hosts was a railroad man, the other a truck driver. Both families lived in small, rural North Dakota communities and they spent summer weekends at their two cottages by the lake. I asked them if they felt that they were missing anything by living in such a sparsely settled corner of the world.

Not at all, they assured me. Big cities had no appeal for them. Winters were cold, sometimes 50 degrees below zero where they lived, but there was no crime in their communities, so they didn't have to lock their doors behind them as people had to do "over in Bismarck."

Kindness, friendliness and generosity, these were the inborn traits of their rural life, the obligations they assumed one to the other and to the occasional strangers who came their way. What surprised me was the resentment they felt towards the native Indians of the area.

"They won't work and they like the government to support them," was the complaint I heard. Then something went out of the afternoon when I heard Indians referred to as "prairie niggers."

I arrived at Garrison Dam the next afternoon after a long, windy, 40-mile trip down the open lake, and tied the boat to a pier in the public park. Then I began to seek assistance in hauling the boat around the two-mile-wide barrier of the dam. A park ranger gave me the telephone number of a man named Elmer. Elmer had a trailer. I called Elmer. His trailer was broken. I called the Corps of Engineers's office at the dam. It was closed.

These calls were made from a public telephone booth at the head of the dock. A fat man, stuffing fistfuls of marshmallows into his mouth, stood outside the hot, cramped booth listening to my calls. He watched my every move as I read through the telephone book and dropped quarter after quarter into the pay slot.

I hated him staring at me, hated his fat sticky fingers and his pink sticky mouth. I hated everything in the park: the plastic coolers, the plastic caps men were wearing, the plastic silver-speckled speedboats tied to the dock with their sound-blasting stereo radios; hated the cars, trailers, trucks and campers jammed in the parking lot. I had returned to civilization after two weeks and 700 miles of solitude and I hated everything about it.

But civilization's equipment was needed to get me over the dam and, call by call, I ran through my diminishing list of of people who might be able to help me. The last name I called was Lee Sailer, a farmer who lived 30 miles south of the dam. The person who answered my call said that Lee and his wife were away visiting relatives and were not expected back until late evening. The voice said she would relay my request for trailer assistance.

Somewhere out there in North Dakota, the future of the voyage hung on a telephone message: a message that would be delivered to a man who would arrive home late on a hot summer night; a message from some damn-fool stranger who wanted his boat hauled over the dam. I was not optimistic as I went to sleep that night.

Early the next mooring, Lee and Mona Sailer (39 years married, four grandchildren, proud farmers from Hazen, North Dakota) backed a truck and trailer down the boat ramp, loaded the *Gander* and hauled us around the dam. Two people, working two hours with their truck and trailer and they were reluctant to charge me $40.

The Missouri became a free-flowing river again below Garrison Dam. This 75-mile section is one of the best remaining natural corridors of the river. It ran with a gentle current, clear and green, around big, easy curves where cows stared out from pastures. Back from the river, houses nestled in clumps of green trees set against a skyline of more green fields. All along the river were hundreds of downed trees, the nighttime work of the many beavers living along the shore.

> Brief note from the Log:
> Today, a wonderful day, wrapped in the ribbon of the curling river.

I reached Bismarck, North Dakota, early in the afternoon and nearly passed through the town before I found a marina where I could tie up. I walked uptown and my expense book recalls what I did in Bismarck: dinner, $9.25; rum, $5.49; gas, $21; cab fare, $5. I remember the dinner because it was at a restaurant that advertised the longest salad bar in North Dakota. The cab fare was because I did not want to walk all the way back to the boat carrying gas cans.

Lake Sakakawea had been big enough. Lake Oahe was even bigger: 231 miles long with a shoreline of 2,250 miles. That distance, I calculated, was longer than the Pacific coastline of the United States, exclusive of Alaska. My charts for the lake covered 33 sheets, each 12 by 18 inches.

The voyage through the lake began pleasantly enough as it carried me past a scenic shoreline of open woods and green farms dotted with white houses and red barns. I made it to a place called Beaver Creek, an idyllic anchorage where I took a sundown walk through a pine forest sprinkled with wildflowers and alive with calling killdeer. The next day, however, was the beginning of an ordeal of space, time and distance that stretched my endurance far beyond what I thought possible.

It was calm the next morning as I started toward Fort Yates, ten miles down the lake and on the opposite shore. I started to cross the two-mile width of the lake just as a light breeze began to blow. At the mid-point of the lake, the boat was walloped by the wind and waves of a sudden half-gale. The flat-bottomed boat was about as seaworthy as a packing crate, so I ran for shelter behind what I thought would be a protecting point and ended up in another forest of ugly, dead snags. It required very careful steering to keep the boat from being smashed by waves against a tree trunk. Dangerous but also an absurd situation that I could be storm-wrecked on a tree in the middle of a lake. Such problems do not occur in the cruising guides to small-boat handling.

Fort Yates, I learned after my safe arrival, is the main town on the Standing Rock Indian Reservation. I passed the burial site of the great Sioux chief, Sitting Bull. He was killed on the reservation in 1890 by US Army soldiers who had come to arrest him. The surviving members of his tribe were moved to the Pine Ridge Reservation in southwest South Dakota. There, they were nearly all killed by the army in the Battle of Wounded Knee. Sadly, the memorial plaque on Sitting Bull's grave said it had been vandalized many times.

The place depressed me. Its main street was lined by three service stations, one grocery store, a small department store featuring Western clothing, a post office, a laundromat and a Burger Queen restaurant. The unemployment rate for the Indians, I was told, was 80 percent. This small, desolate place was all that was left to a people who, long ago, owned it all.

The summer gale kept me from leaving Fort Yates. I was amazed by the size and frequency of the waves rolling northward. With a hundred-mile fetch for the waves to form, the lake heaved and rolled like an inland sea. Wind-bound, I had to use my imagination to plan a day of nothing. Each small task had to be done so as to make it last. I cleaned all my pans and dishes, aired my sleeping bag and washed my clothes. Then I made elaborate preparations for lunch, set the table with a bouquet of flowers, and sat down as a guest of one to eat my standard lunch of crackers, peanut butter and raisins. Catching up on notes and a nap got me through to five o'clock. Then I gave up and had dinner at the Burger Queen.

The following morning was calm and I was able to leave Fort Yates. The next two days, running down the length of Lake Oahe, were the most difficult and trying of the entire voyage.

Notes from the Log:

Slow going down from Fort Yates to Mobridge through miles of flooded, standing trees and underwater stumps, ugly brown-gray shapes lurking just below the surface of the water. Any one of them — and there are thousands — could smash a hole in the bottom of the boat. There are more of them along the shore I hug where the possibility of being rammed is greater. But I hold this line because if the boat were holed, I would at least have a chance of swimming to shore. It is the constant and intense examination of the small area just ahead of the boat that exhausts me. I begin to see things that do not exist, imagined shapes that lurk in the murky water. Fifty miles and ten hours later, I reach Mobridge, an eye-strained, whipped river traveler.

Mobridge is the sports-fishing center for Lake Oahe. It is more of a cult than a sport, I thought, as I sat for the evening among the fishing boats tied to a dock, a cult with its own language, rituals, symbols and equipment. I was astounded by the technology of the cult; the boats were equipped with high-speed engines, depth sounders, fish-scanning screens, out-rigger poles, fresh-water bait tanks, pivoting seats and auxiliary electric trolling engines. All this, I thought, for a fish. Fish talk was all I heard as each man held up the chain-linked body count of his day's catch for the triumphant photograph. Scorned them, yes, but secretly hoped that one of the men would throw me a fresh fish for dinner.

Notes from the Log:

Mobridge to Oahe Dam. Perfectly calm day but hot. Under way by 6:15 A.M. Arrived Oahe Dam 115 miles and 15 hours later. This was a day that was too long, too hot, on a lake so big that I travel on it in a kind of hallucinatory exhaustion. I make short stops to break the monotony, stop for lunch, stop for a nap, stop for a swim. But the lake is still there, on and on and on. No logs to dodge, no wind; nothing to divert my mind from the tedium of this slow passage.

Feet so sunburned and swollen from standing that I can only crawl when I go into the cabin for the bottle of rum courage. Make this day, I tell myself, and I can do anything.

Late in the afternoon, I reached a place called Little Bend where the lake curves around a long, narrow, seven-mile peninsula. It took me nearly three hours to travel the 14 miles around the peninsula and when I completed the circuit, I was less than a quarter of a mile across the land from where I had started.

I stopped in a little cove for dinner after 12 hours of continuous running. My back ached from standing so long, and I was exhausted. I was having a drink in the cockpit when I noticed a moth fluttering helplessly on the lake. Its wings beat on the skin of the water, stopped, fluttered again, and then the moth lay still. I was so tired I could barely sit up, but I was alive and the moth was dying.

Reluctantly I put down my drink, took off my pants and jumped into the water to save the moth. I waded ashore to a little sand spit where I placed the moth on the beach and watched it crawl up the sand, dragging its sodden wings behind it. Its track crossed the various colors of sand and rock that lined the beach. In those lines, crossed by a limping moth, was etched the lake's long history of flood and storm. Wading back to the boat, I looked down in the clear water and saw a single white stone lying on the bottom.

I reached for the rock and kept it, a memento of the place and the moment. In the log, I wrote:

Here, where I saved the life of an insignificant moth by a small sand spit that reveals all the history of the lake, I feel I have

100

reached the center of my voyage. I have passed over the line of who and where I have been to live solely within the boat, on the river and for the miles yet to travel.

Oahe Dam was a little sliver of light across a dark river when I arrived there, late in the evening. Far away on a distant hill, the headlights of one lone car followed along the line of an invisible highway. A single arc light in the middle of an empty parking lot greeted my arrival at the boat ramp above the dam. I had arrived at nowhere.

In the morning, I walked two miles downriver to the Oahe Marina and started telephone negotiations for a haul over the dam. It was Sunday and the commercial places I called were all closed. Hope hung on the return call of an equipment dealer who, someone told me, might be able to do the job. While I waited, I read week-old newspapers in the marina office. "Something will turn up," everyone assured me. And it did. The marina manager remembered an old equipment trailer parked on a farm a few miles east of the dam. Together, we drove across the fields of South Dakota looking for a farmer and his trailer. We found both, hitched up the trailer, loaded the boat and by early afternoon I was back on the river heading for Pierre, the capital of South Dakota.

Pierre's waterfront is a long lakeside park of green lawns, picnic areas and playgrounds. I arrived there on a Sunday afternoon and the park was filled with people. I went ashore for a walk, watched a ball game, sat in on a religious meeting, viewed an art exhibit and listened to a concert. In all of this, I was a detached spectator, so different from the continuous and concentrated experience of traveling the river. There, in the park, I could turn left, turn right or sit down. It was an empty freedom, this being able to do as I pleased, compared to my boat life where the river dictated my every moment. Feeling a part of nothing as I walked the Sunday afternoon in that park, I also felt lonely, a feeling I had never had traveling through the lonely country of Montana, and North and South Dakota. Late in the afternoon I returned to the familiar, small world of my boat; I was at home again, and ready to go on down Lake Sharpe, the 80-mile-long lake backed up behind Big Bend Dam.

Notes from the Log:

Twelve-hour day running Lake Sharpe to Big Bend Dam. Southeast headwinds all day. Today, (day 21) I reached the mid-point in the voyage down the Missouri River; a thousand miles behind me, a thousand miles to go.

I marked that place of a thousand miles with a red bandana; I tied it to a broken tree at an unnamed point of empty land on the Stanley County shore of Lake Sharpe in south-central South Dakota on a windy June morning at 10:35 A.M. For me, there was something special in the idea that I had made a voyage of a thousand miles. It was an old ambition, a voyage of this length — the miles had to be earned through effort and endurance and always, the outcome had to hang in doubt. That red bandana marked the achievement of that ambition and, at a thousand miles, I had crossed a line. No longer was I the semi-educated dilettante, the comfortable, middle-aged man of home, garden and loving wife. These things I had been — a thousand miles ago — but now, as I quoted earlier, I was only what the river had made me: a whiskered, mud-caked, sun-burnt man determined to go down this god-damned twisting brown river for another thousand miles or leave my bones along its shores.

By luck, I made an easy portage around Big Bend Dam with the assistance of a park ranger and, by mid-morning of the next day, I reached Chamberlain, South Dakota. I arrived in a downpour of rain that dumped seven inches in just a few hours. I took shelter in the city library and read a book covering the early pioneer settlements of the area. Later, the weather cleared, and on an evening warm and fresh-smelling after the storm, I went on down the river and anchored the boat in a small cove.

Were I asked to quickly recall a particular image of the voyage, the scene that would instantly come to mind would be that evening below Chamberlain. In the library, I had read the histories of the people who had settled the area. The small dramas of their lives had consisted of ordinary striving, modest successes and many failures, and their histories had strangely affected me. I pulled the boat into the shore of the cove and walked to the top of a small hill overlooking the soft, rolling South Dakota prairie lands with green grass and wildflowers in every direction. I was looking at land; land as life, land as a story of families and communities, formed and reformed through birth and death by generations of farming families. The boat radio had picked up a concert that filled the cove with music. In a mood of great contentment, I sat all that June evening on that hill watching the land disappear in the dark of a warm night and then reappear under a full moon.

A tail wind followed me the next day down the 107-mile length of Lake Francis Case. It was not dangerous but it created waves that lifted the stern high enough for the propeller to spin in the air. I was forced to go slowly, and took 13 hours to reach Fort Randall Dam at the lower end of the lake. I arrived in a coma of fatigue, stumbled up a steep hillside to reach a highway, and walked three miles before I found a get-and-go food store with a telephone. The girl clerk knew nothing about anyone, anywhere. All she could do was sell me — in the middle of one of the world's greatest beef regions — a blob of tasteless meat she called a hamburger. In between calls, I had to listen to the store's loudly amplified, twanging western music.

My telephone calls finally connected with a man named Sam who promised to show up the next morning with his truck to haul the boat over the dam. True to his word, Sam showed up the next morning with a huge farm truck, its bed a full five feet above ground.

"Won't work, Sam," I said as he backed the truck down the boat ramp. "Bed's too high out of the water to get the boat on it."

Sam, in farmer overalls and straw hat, looked at the boat, pulled out a length of cable from his truck-mounted winch and said, "Sonny, stand aside. I can move anything that ain't tied to the ground."

One of the ropes I carried on the boat was an old climbing rope, a type of rope that has considerable stretch. We tied the rope to the boat, then to a hook on Sam's winch and he started winding it up. The rope stretched and stretched but the boat did not move. Then it stretched some more and the boat shot up the ramp onto the back of Sam's truck.

"I ain't never seen a rope like that," said the amazed Sam. "It's like a rubber band."

Two hours later he slipped the boat into the fast-moving water below the dam. We chatted for a while, and Sam said, "Been wanting to take a trip down the river all my life. Something I've never gotten around to doing."

Finally, I asked him what I owed him.

"What's it worth to you?" asked Sam.

"Anything you ask," I replied. "Without your help, my trip would have ended back there above the dam."

"Well," he said, "that there truck cost me $25,000 and I been hauling your boat most of the morning. How about you giving me that rope and we call it square."

Sam, whatever your last name, from somewhere in South Dakota, I can only thank you with these words: people like you were the best part of the journey.

The Missouri ran as a river again below Fort Randall Dam before it became Lewis and Clark Lake. Its natural corridor was a relief after the arid bleakness of the big lakes and life returned to its shores. Deer, browsing in small groups, froze at my appearance and watched my passage with large, limpid eyes, only an ear twitching in their otherwise immobile stance. Summer cottages on green islands of grass could be seen through the trees, and people waved friendly greetings as I passed. I was in a relaxed and restful mood as I came to the head of Lewis and Clark Lake, the last of the big Missouri River lakes.

The head of the lake covers a wide marshland; somewhere I lost the main channel and found myself wandering through its shallow waters. There were hundreds of possible leads, each lined by tall cattails that prevented me from seeing where I was going. The area was too shallow to run the motor, so I waded through it, towing the boat. It was such a lovely marsh, with birds, luxuriant grasses and bright red flowers, that I enjoyed my hour as I pushed and poled my way through the maze.

Notes from the Log:
Ran the short 25-mile length of Lewis and Clark Lake today, looking across to the Nebraska shore. Arrived Gavins Point Dam

at 8:30 P.M. to conclude the 1,263-mile run of the great lakes of the Missouri. To celebrate, I clean up. Shave with my smoking pipe clenched in my teeth as I squint into a small bit of broken mirror. Then a dousing of after-shave lotion and the inside of the boat smells like a barber shop. After that, I don my go-ashore blue blazer with brass buttons, now wrinkled and dusty, but appropriate wear for an after-dinner cocktail party of one with the same old rum.

That night, in the marina at Gavins Point Dam, I laid away the charts of the upper Missouri. On each were scribbled my comments, observations, figures and curses. Together, they were the written thoughts of a man talking to himself on charts that were sometimes flapping in the wind, sometimes soggy with rain. The upper Missouri with its shallows, sandbars, hidden stumps and drowned forests, was behind me. The Missouri just a few miles downstream was a commercially navigable river that followed a dredged and marked channel all the way to St. Louis, 850 miles away. For the first time, I felt that I might even get there.

But Old Muddy wasn't through with me yet. The next day, the river below the dam was rising and I rode the edge of the flood down to Sioux City, Iowa. Floating logs, limbs and brush picked up by the high water accumulated at points to build dams ten feet high that projected part way across the river. Currents piled up behind these dams, searched for openings and raced around the ends of the tangled wreckage. Below the driftwood dams, the water made great sucking and slurping sounds as it turned back upstream in great circling eddies. Out in the channel, a safe distance from collapsing river banks, I rode the back of a twisting, slithering, green-brown snake, along with its floating logs, plastic bottles, piles of sticks, limbs and thick mats of dead grass.

CHAPTER SIX

COUNTING BACKWARDS, MILE 734 TO 0

A T SIOUX CITY, 734 MILES upstream from the Missouri's mouth, I entered the river's dredged and marked navigation channel. No more sandbars to trip on, no more snags lurking beneath the water to ram the boat. Ahead lay a man-made channel 300 feet wide and nine feet deep through which currents would be running from two to seven miles an hour. Along this channel, each mile would be posted on a marker board. Navigating this river section, I thought, could become a bit monotonous. All I would have to do was keep the boat in the middle of the channel, pay attention to my 139-page-long chart book and count backwards from 734 to 0.

All the ornery wildness had been taken out of the Missouri. I felt as though I had come down out of the mountains and the plains to civilization. Rounding a bend below Sioux City, I drifted past a mile of car bodies, crushed and rusting, that had been pushed over the river bank to form a rip-rap wall of junk. At the Lighthouse

106

Marina restaurant, I had to wear a tie and jacket to be served dinner. At Decatur, Nebraska, I spent a sleepless night listening to the din of a shore-side rock concert.

I stopped for lunch at Cottonwood Marina, a small community of trailer houses, boats, restaurants and gift shops. Couples sat under little Cinzano umbrellas, eating and drinking. I felt terribly out of place as I sat in the mud-caked boat eating my peanut butter-raisin lunch, a single man with a week's growth of whiskers in a place where people came as clean, domestic couples.

The high water had flooded hundreds of acres of low cornfields and the river was littered with thousands of stalks. It was impossible to avoid them. They would wrap around the shaft of the outboard and every ten minutes or so, I had to shut the engine off, lift it out of the water and untangle the stalks with a knife.

That high water carried me to Omaha, Nebraska, where I waited for it to drop from a high crest of 22 feet. There, I met Lonnie and "Peaches" Morrow who lived on the river in a houseboat-cruiser. He had brought the cruiser upriver from St. Louis to Omaha, a trip he said he would never make again. Pushing against the current all the way, he had burned a thousand gallons of gas, bent both his engine shafts and lost both propellers.

I left Omaha on a hot afternoon, the temperature hovering close to 100 degrees, and anchored that night in the mouth of the Platte River. "Too thick to drink and too thin to plow" goes the old saw about the Platte. I tested the "too thick to drink" part and proved it wrong by the medicinal addition of a shot of rum I mixed with its muddy water.

Notes from the Log:
Cool the dawn and the river runs slowly, strong and silvered. I awake to a day of promises and expectations. By evening, it is different. The day of 117 miles of travel in 104-degree weather has scorched and battered me with its hot winds. At a leafy green inlet without a name, I stopped for a swim in cool green water beneath cool green trees. I swam around the boat, checking for damage, naked and floating in the water. In the evening, I haul my tired body into the cabin and lie on the bunk. Rum and

orange juice is all I can manage for food. Surviving a day like this, I think, gives me the right to claim the company of others who have traveled this river long before me, along its twin shores of heat, wind and dust.

The glittering morning skyline of Kansas City, Missouri, came into view as I rounded a bend at mile marker 366. The chart showed the location of a waterfront park where I tied up. I also needed gas and I figured a local person might be found who would drive me to the nearest gas station. I waited for an hour or so at the park dock, rather surprised that no one had driven by. I then walked up to the park entry and found it gated and locked. The posted sign read "Chemical Contamination. Keep Out." I swam no more in the Missouri below Kansas City.

At the little community of Waverly, I faced the grim prospect of a long, hot walk up a hill and into the town to get gas. A kindly old gentleman in a dusty, wheezing car offered me a ride. Before we got to the town, his car ran out of gas. I got out, trudged up the hill, filled my tank and on the way back down, poured half my hard-earned gas into his car.

At Booneville, Missouri, I sat out a humid afternoon at the Booneville Fisherman's Club. It consisted of benches and tables beneath the shade of a tree. The old men of the club, both black and white, had fashioned the club's furniture out of salvaged boxes and planks. Each and every day, they told me, they came to "their club" to fish, smoke, talk, drink beer and argue. Every river city, I thought, should have a Booneville Fisherman's Club, a place for men to sit out their old age.

I was reaching the end of the long voyage down the Missouri and there was not much of me left to see or think or feel. On that last stretch, the connecting links of miles and hours seemed to be all pushed together in a muddle of heat and miles of unchanging shoreline.

I felt dirty and I couldn't bathe in the river. I had not even touched it below Kansas City. My feet were swollen and fly-bitten, hair matted and gritty. The thermometer read 103 degrees and everything I touched was hot. The river ran on and on as it had for the last 500 miles between two thin parallel lines of trees that hid the flat farmlands beyond. I tried to think "inside" my head, tried to fall into meditations that blotted out the future of the miles yet to go and the heat-bright sameness of the river.

Below the Gasconade River, the shoreline of the Missouri became steep and topped out in a series of remarkably green terraces and bluffs. I had entered the Rhineland of the Missouri and the little town of Hermann was its capital. The town — Old World schmaltz and gingerbread ornamentation — was celebrating its 150th birthday when I arrived. In the cool cellar of the Hermannhof vineyards I sat, surrounded by dark casks dripping beaded moisture, and sipped wine. Then, after a huge German dinner, I strolled along streets with such honored names as Mozart, Schiller and Guttenberg.

My last night on the Missouri was spent in the old river town of St. Charles. It was from there, on May 21, 1804, that the Lewis and Clark expedition set out on its long trek up the Missouri and down the Columbia to cross North America. Had I been there on that historic morning, and knowing what I do about the route that lay ahead for the expedition, I would have advised them not to go.

On the next day — my 36th on the river — under a full moon and a rising sun, I came to the end of the Missouri, and *Gander* and I floated out on the waters of the Mississippi. I called my wife and was able to give to her the same report Lewis and Clark gave to President Jefferson on their return from coming back down the Missouri: "The thing is done."

Chapter Seven

TO CHICAGO AND GEORGIAN BAY

PREPARATIONS FOR THE LAST leg of the voyage were altogether different from the planning efforts that went into the journeys on the Columbia and Missouri: no boat to build, test and outfit, no long truck-and-trailer haul to make. I packed an overnight bag and flew to St. Louis to begin the concluding and complicated 1,600-mile route across the continent. It would carry me north on the Mississippi, up the Illinois River to Chicago, and then up and around Lake Michigan to Lake Huron and around Georgian Bay. There, the route would turn southeasterly and cross Ontario, Canada, through the Trent-Severn Canal to Lake Ontario and the St. Lawrence River. Then it would lead down the St. Lawrence, up the Richelieu River to Lake Champlain and down the Champlain Canal to the Hudson River to New York City and the Atlantic. Charts for this long, intricate route would have been very expensive so for most of it, I relied on road maps and pages from old *National Geographic* magazines.

I had stored the boat for the winter in a shed at Portage des Sioux, upriver from St. Louis on the Mississippi. The Mississippi had risen to near record flood levels and the boat had floated and been pinned under the roof of the shed. I found it undamaged but full of mud, sticks, leaves and thousands of crawling ants. After two days of cleaning, the ants and I went up the Mississippi and entered the Illinois River.

The 320-mile-long Illinois River with its six locks was the critical link in the overland water route, connecting the Mississippi River with Lake Michigan. The connection was made by diverting the flow of the Chicago River away from Lake Michigan and into a canal leading to the Illinois.

Recent rains had raised the level of the river and I fought persistent currents as I pushed up the green-flowing river. For long, tedious miles, nothing broke the monotony of the low, flooded, tree-lined shore. Temperature and humidity both read 90. "Be where you are" — the mental discipline I had tried to follow on the Missouri — was not working on this river. At the beginning of the Illinois, I wanted it to end.

On the second day on the river, I went through the first lock which lifted me ten feet to the level of La Grange Pool: same scenery, same flooded farmlands, same opposing current, same heat and humidity. Lunch that day was a sandwich filled with a gooey paste of cucumbers gone to mush in the heat. But the ants were mostly gone, victims of the traps I had made by pouring sugary breakfast cereal on pieces of paper placed in corners of the boat. When the papers became covered with ants, I threw them overboard. Now, I no longer had to brush them out of the bunk, skim them out of drawers and shelves or pick them out of my dinner.

Peoria, Illinois, was my first view of a Midwestern industrial city. Huge factories towered above me as I passed along the Peoria waterfront, each of them spitting out steam, smoke, noise and smells through pipes, stacks, vents, outfalls and drainage ditches. Who, I wondered, designed such incredible complexes of machinery and buildings? Ugly, brutal and yet fascinating were those masses of iron, steel and concrete.

To me, slowly floating by, those places seemed to be work prisons without joy or beauty, where life was exchanged for a wage. It made me thank whatever lucky chance or twist of fate it was that allowed me to be on the river instead of a worker on that shore. I suppose that the kind of fellow who spends much of his life working around boats and dreaming of voyages sees to it that he insulates himself from life's drudgeries. He might be impractical, a bit of dreamer, but he has larger ambitions for his life than to spend it working in a factory. I was lucky; I had had those rivermen in my early life to emulate, who lived outside the narrow restraints of the conventional, work-day world. The work they did, they chose to do. Not easy nor very well rewarded, never secure and sometimes dangerous: it was a way of life for those men, rather than something called a job. My work, like theirs, was with boats and the river and because of them, I was there on a boat drifting by that industrial prison, not in it.

A large lake fronts the city of Peoria, formed by the dam across the Illinois below the city. I anchored for the night in a snug cove in this lake but around midnight, I awoke to a raging storm of wind, rain and lightning. The anchor could not hold the boat and it grounded in a marsh of mud and grass. Naked, I jumped overboard and pushed it deeper into the grass. Laughing somewhat hysterically in the driving wind and rain, I held the boat until the storm passed, a human anchor, muck-covered and drenched.

The following day, the river was carrying the runoff of the rainstorm and my speed was reduced to a crawl. The flood waters carried huge amounts of driftwood, sticks, branches, and rafts of grass. It seemed as though the lower part of the outboard was a magnet that gathered this material around its shaft. The only way to clear it was to stop the engine, tilt the shaft out of the water and then unstring it by hand. Ten minutes later, I would have to repeat the process again and, without the engine running, the boat would drift back downstream on the fast current.

At Bandon Road Dam, just below Joliet, Illinois, water was released from the dam as a seething flood of white foam that carried with it the nose-burning smell of strong chemicals. The shoreline above the dam was a continuous line of junkyards piled high with rusting cars and trucks, and abandoned machinery. The last lock on the Illinois lifted me up to the industrial moat of the Chicago Sanitary Canal, lined by slime-brown cement walls. Six inches of foam covered the water and long strands of plastic sheeting trailed behind the boat.

It was the Saturday of a three-day holiday. All the factories were closed and surrounded by acres of black, empty parking lots. I did not see any people but the factories — as though they had a life of their own — emitted vaporous clouds of hissing steam and belches of black smoke. The only life I saw was the bright clumps of daisies rooted in cracks in the canals and over them, the tented nests of crawling caterpillars.

Late in the afternoon, I turned into what is called the Calumet Sag Canal, spotted a tiny opening in the cement wall of the canal, and backed the boat in for the night under a canopy of trees. It was my first anchorage in a sewer outfall. The smell was bad enough but worse was the realization that I was floating in a stagnant, warm pool of filth. There, I spent the night listening to the background roar of traffic on the outskirts of the great city of Chicago. In the morning, the boat was surrounded by a thin, gaseous layer of fog-like vapor hovering just above the green-black surface of the pool. I hauled in the anchor to get away from the place as quickly as I could and it surfaced with long strands of green, slimy weeds wrapped around its hooks.

From the Chicago Sanitary Canal, the Calumet Sag Canal runs east as a dredged ditch for 16 miles. For three hours, I ran the straight line of that ditch between twin shores of piled dirt and rock gouged out of the earth to form the channel. It was an utterly boring and depressing passage that led me to the even more depressing place called Calumet City on the Little Calumet River.

My map showed a place on the river marked "Yacht Club." Great, I thought, a bit of yachting camaraderie, a shower, a drink on the terrace and then dinner. The "club" turned out to be a deserted collection of ramshackle docks and shacks bounded by railroad tracks. Two other marinas refused my request to tie up and

I was about ready to search for another sewer outlet for the night when I found a friendly place called Skipper's Marina where I was able to moor.

I spent five days at Skipper's Marina, waiting for the winds to die down on Lake Michigan. Five days in a tavern near the dock with a group of unemployed steel workers playing cards and the pinball machines, drinking beer, eating nothing but pizza and listening to high-volume western music. When the tavern closed at night, the owner piped the music out over the dock so I wouldn't feel "lonely."

I wanted to get going; wanted to shake off the feeling of dirtiness that had enveloped the boat and me since we entered the Chicago Sanitary Canal. Everyone warned me, however, to stay off the lake. Said one boatman, "You wouldn't have a chance out there if you hit a storm. It's not a lake, it's a god-damned ocean."

My plan had been to travel up the eastern shore of the lake and stop at the little ports along the way. The problem was that some of these ports were 30 miles apart. Most boats would be able to cover that distance in a few hours. For *Gander*, however, a 30-mile run between ports would take six hours and that was too long a time to be exposed to the possibility of a sudden storm on the lake. Regretfully, I started looking for a truck, trailer and driver for a haul around Lake Michigan. What followed were the two absolute low points of the voyage.

Andy Webster, who operated a marine service in Calumet City, agreed to haul the boat if I could find a trailer. I fed quarters into a pay phone for an entire morning, calling boatyards, marinas and trailer-rental outlets. No one had a trailer for rent large enough for a 24-foot boat. It was a ridiculous predicament. At all the remote dams along the Missouri, I had always been able to find a trailer for a portage but in the great city of Chicago, nothing.

Finally, I located a boating store whose manager said he would sell me a used trailer for $400 and refund me $200 if I returned it. It was robbery but I had no choice. Andy and I drove out to get the rig. It was a wreck, all the tires flat and no lights. We made what repairs we had to, loaded the boat, and headed out on the freeway during the Friday afternoon traffic.

Fifty miles north of Chicago, the trailer collapsed. I will never forget the horror of the next few hours. We were trapped on a very narrow shoulder of the highway with just inches of space between us and the roar of hundreds of passing trucks. The trailer had to be raised so we could repair it but the jack did not give enough lift. I piled all the books from my library under it. Still too short. Then I pulled up all the boat's floorboards and added them to the pile of books and we were able to repair the trailer. We drove all night to reach St. Ignace on Lake Huron, just across the Mackinac Bridge.

The worst was yet to come.

Andy was making a slow, wide turn to back the boat down the ramp at St. Ignace when there was a loud crash behind us. We looked behind. The boat and the trailer had tipped over and both lay on their sides on the parking lot, still tied together. It was an awful moment. I could not see the underside of the boat but I assumed it had been smashed. Another voyage ending, not on a river but in a parking lot, I thought. However, the good luck that had taken me this far was still with me.

A construction crew of eight men, working on the highway, heard the crash and came over to investigate. Without having to be asked, they took hold of the bottom edge of the boat and, together, gave a great lift that righted both the boat and the trailer. The inside of the boat was a mess of books, groceries, equipment and broken dishes but the outside was barely scratched. We launched the boat. Andy promised to return the trailer and send me the refund (he did) and drove back to Chicago. *Gander* and I, with the mess below, headed out into a bright, sunlit day toward the inviting green of Mackinac Island in the far western corner of Lake Huron.

Boat and I needed a rest stop, a time for cleaning up after the long, hot, muggy and dirty crawl up the Illinois, the grime of Chicago and Calumet City and the debacle of the trailer accident. The clean, white-painted and quiet 19th-century village on Mackinac Island was just what I was looking for. I stayed on the boat the entire afternoon of my arrival, cleaning up, while listening to nothing louder than the clip-clop of horses' hooves because motorized vehicles are banned from the island.

In the evening I walked up to the century-old Grand Hotel over-looking the town and the harbor. I thought I was looking very "yachty" in my blue blazer and my only clean tennis shoes so, bravely, I walked the length of its colonnaded porch, past small tables where guests sipped drinks and talked, swept imperiously past the hotel doorman, crossed the deep-carpeted lobby, and plunked myself down on a barstool to drink an iced gin and bitters. Later, I attended the Michigan Bach Festival celebrating the hotel's centennial. Altogether, it was an elegant evening ashore for the captain of a scow, late of a Calumet sewer anchorage.

Two days later, I left Mackinac Island and traveled eastward through the lovely Les Cheneaux Islands and then turned north to Thessalon, Ontario, the most northerly point on the overland water route. There, I cleared Canadian customs, stocked up on food and gas, and headed eastward again through the 190-mile-long North Channel.

Notes from the Log:
At anchor in a calendar-art picture cove on Bassett Island, halfway through North Channel. Around me lies the downed forest of beaver-cut birch trees. The little varmints are everywhere and they pay no attention to me as they swim around the anchored boat. Their mounds are huge, six and eight feet high, standing like hay stacks around the perimeter of the bay. Above me, in wind-sighing trees, hundreds of small birds twitter and sing.

The next day was a 75-mile run through the exquisite red and pink islands of Whaleback Channel with the rise of the La Cloche Mountains a distant blue horizon to the north. The visual contrasts of this passage were staggering. I went through the narrow channel of Little Current, barely a few hundred feet wide, then out into the sparkling waters of Manitowaning Bay, past a chain of clustered islands, and then through an opening that revealed the ocean-like horizon of Georgian Bay. In the twilight of that day, I arrived at the small community of Killarney in the northernmost corner of Georgian Bay. I had been under way since dawn and I was too tired to hunt out a public moorage, so I stopped at the first dock I came to. A group of women were eating dinner at the far end of the dock. One of them came over to the boat.

"Welcome to George Island," she said. "I'm Ann and we're having a party." With that introduction, she handed me a glass of cold champagne and said, "Stay for the night. You are my first guest of the year and the first guest does not have to pay."

I stayed two days with Ann in Killarney, where she is known by her Ojibwa Indian name which she spelled for me, *Cabatokocheshosme.* Translated, she said, it means "The Lady Who Walks on the Hill with the Wind in Her Hair."

One day, I went with Ann and her friend, Willy, an Ojibwa Indian, in Willy's boat, *Quack Quack,* to see what he said was a sacred island. Willy stayed in the boat while Ann and I climbed a rocky path to the island's high summit. Around us were uncountable islands and long, finger-like peninsulas, green-black under their unbroken forest canopies. Off to the south, almost floating in the clarity of the spring sunshine, loomed the soft contours of the La Cloche Mountains. I felt that Willy and The Lady Who Walks on the Hill with the Wind in Her Hair had taken me, a stranger, into a special, hidden and secret place of that high northern lake country. And I like to think it was on that hill that Ann got her name, and that old Willy was the one who gave it to her.

Before leaving Killarney, I bought a cruising guide and a package of charts for Georgian Bay. In the evening, as I lay anchored in Beaverstone Bay, 25 miles east of Killarney, I used the charts and the book to study the route ahead. There were ten sheets of charts. Laid end-to-end, those sheets would have made a continuous chart 40 feet long. To get an overall picture of the passage, I laid them out on the bunks and the floor and taped sections to the cabin windows and walls.

Each chart portrayed a fractured coastline of deep, twisting inlets and an offshore bank of thousands upon thousands of rocks and islands. Through it all, like a slalom course, ran the red line of the navigable channel defined by some 500 buoys and markers. Names stood out, descriptive of possible hazards: Turnaway

Rock, Obstacle Island, Hole in the Wall, Shoal Narrows and Hang Dog Reef. The word "Caution" stood out in bold type on many of the pages:

Caution — This section of the route leads through waters which are incompletely sounded.

Caution — It is especially important, because of many shoals, that the mariner should proceed only when sure of his position.

Caution — Great care should be taken in these waters because the water is almost opaque making shoal water difficult to detect until close to it.

To these rather alarming warnings was added the cruising guide's stern rules for navigating the channel:

It is absolutely essential when piloting the route to identify and count all the islands as you pass them, as well as the beacons and buoys. If you lose your place on the chart or the water you might make a disastrous wrong turn. In effect, one pilots with a finger on the chart tracing the course and each of its marks, spotting the next aid well before arrival.

What concerned me as I studied the charts were the two hops that required long offshore passages in order to skirt two large areas of rocks and reefs. The guidebook warned that these passages were entirely unsheltered, that they could be hazardous in heavy seas, and that small craft should not attempt them unless weather and visibility were good. The first of these passages involved my next day's travel south from Beaverstone Bay.

I awoke the next morning to fog, wind and the sound of waves breaking at the outer entrance to the bay. I had to know what it was like out on Georgian Bay, so cautiously I poked out through the entrance of the bay and ran a short distance out. Immediately, fog blotted out the shoreline behind me and the boat bounced and rolled in the peaks and hollows of gray, lumpy waves. Not today, I decided, and I ran back to the shelter of the bay and tied the boat to the rocky edge of a tiny island.

For two days, that little island was my home. My steps memorized it, blindfolded I could have walked it: 20 steps left to a stunted forest of 16 small trees; 31 steps up to its rocky promontory, there to listen to the call of the loon and the gong of an offshore buoy that marked the slow crawl of time.

Lightning and thunder awoke me on my third morning in Beaverstone Bay. The surface of the bay was dimpled by heavy rain. The fog had lifted but the wind still blew. I dreaded the prospect of another long day of doing nothing, so I turned to the chart to see if there was any alternative to the exposed route to the south. The main channel ran three miles straight out from the shore to clear a dangerous cluster of rocks called "The Chickens." Then, the channel made a 90-degree turn to follow an exposed offshore line south for 28 miles. The line, for most of its length was seven miles out from the shore in the open waters of Georgian Bay. What the line cleared, in addition to The Chickens, was an incredible number of rocks and reefs that fly-specked the shore. On the chart, the seaward edge of this band of rocks was marked with the warning "Breaks in heavy seas."

Then the thought occurred to me that a course that could somehow sneak along the shore inside The Chickens and all the other outlying rocks and islands would be protected by the islands themselves. Was such a passage possible, I wondered, even in a shallow-draft boat like *Gander*? I balanced another day of doing nothing against the effort of an attempt and headed out to thread my way through the shattered maze of The Chickens.

Crossing them, I sometimes waded across rock shelves, towing the boat behind me. In other places, I poled my way along with an oar. Never did I know my exact location. What I did know was that somewhere to my right were the open waters of Georgian Bay and somewhere to my left was the mainland. My navigational philosophy was simple: I just had to keep wading and poling and eventually I would arrive somewhere.

At last I broke out of The Chickens, started the engine, and headed across a wide bay. Halfway across the bay, fog moved in and visibility was reduced to only a few yards. In the fog, I knew I could run up on a rock nearly awash before I could see it and a holed boat was suddenly a very real possibility. And what then? A quick glance at the chart showed the frightening outcome of such a disaster. The land inshore of me was a large island, roadless and uninhabited. Assuming I could swim to it, I would then have a bush walk of three miles to the other side of the island, a swim across another channel to the mainland, and then a 30-mile walk to the nearest highway.

By luck, the fog cleared for a moment, and in that moment of visibility, I was able to see a clear passage ahead that led to a sheltered cove. I named the place "Thank God Cove." The fog lifted in the afternoon and I made my way across the Maitland Bank, another rock field called "The Fingerboard," and then called it a day.

Note from the Log:
Something of a record today; 12 hours to travel 11 miles.

The next day, I followed the charted passage that turned inland through a protected but tortuous route that twisted and curved around hundreds of islands. It took me two tries to steer through the rock-blasted, 90-degree turn called "Parting Channel," so named, said the guidebook, because it is "where the brave and the timid part company." The buoyed route continued to zig and zag through the most intricate waterway imaginable. At one place, I somehow rounded a corner, turned around, and without knowing it, started backtracking along the way I had come. From then on, I put a check mark beside each buoy as I passed it so as to keep on the track.

Late in the afternoon, the passage led me back to the misty and windy waters of Georgian Bay. The next ten miles was another exposed, offshore section with, said the guidebook, "rocks and reefs lying close to the channel on both sides." It advised that the passage should not be attempted unless weather and visibility were good. Weather and visibility were not good, so I ran back to Gereaux Island where the lighthouse keeper gave me permission to tie up for the night. He then invited me for supper and on the way to his house, he, with his dog leading the way, took me on a little tour around his island home.

Proudly, he showed me the flower beds that followed various paths radiating out from his house. These beds, he told me, were the work of his wife who had recently died. She had created the garden on the rocky island by bringing soil from the mainland in baskets. Every night he made the same walk around the island with his dog, pausing each time at the small grave where his wife's ashes were buried. All the time we walked, he talked, telling me he had retired as a bricklayer, then joined the Canadian Coast Guard and been posted to the lighthouse of Gereaux Island. We returned to the house and his talking continued. I was just a stranger who had stopped by and so, he said, "It doesn't make any difference what I tell you because you will be gone tomorrow and we will never meet again."

Long into the night he continued telling me his story, revealing the most intimate details, the dreams and disappointments of a life. Day and night made no difference to him; he lived in a solitary world of no time. We had dinner again at midnight and breakfast at three in the morning. Just before dawn, he picked up a weather report that forecast a drop in the wind. He made another breakfast and asked me to stay over another day.

It was a sad leaving and, looking behind as I pulled away, I saw him and his dog taking one more walk around his island, past the abandoned flower garden, past the grave of his wife: a walk of memories he had shared with me during a night of storm on one of the outer islands of Georgian Bay. And saddest of all was the future he dreaded. The lighthouse was soon to be closed. Then he would have to leave the island and move ashore to someplace with no memories at all.

"Coward," I kept telling myself, "a mile isn't very far. Keep to the course."

The course was directly away from the shore, now invisible behind me in the thin light of dawn, and I had a very lonely feeling out there as boat and I crashed into the waves of yesterday's storm. Somewhere ahead of me was the buoy I was looking for, the buoy that would turn me south for ten offshore miles and then lead me to the protection of the next inlet. I wanted to put the passage behind me, wanted to quit worrying about fog, wind, waves and rocks. Two hours and ten buoys later, I passed through the narrow opening of Alexander Passage and in a sudden change of scenery, I traveled along a domesticated and landscaped shoreline of large, turn-of-the-century summer homes.

I spent the next three warm and sunny days slowly wandering through the twisting inside passages of Georgian Bay, still marking off each buoy as I passed it. There were a few small settlements and a passing architectural showcase of splendid and elegant summer homes and cabins. Too soon, I reached the southern end of Georgian Bay, the end of the 40 feet of charts, the last of the 500 buoys and the last island in the chain of thousands. And, tired as I was at the end of this magnificent passage, I would gladly have turned around and run it all over again. Instead, I pulled into Port Severn and prepared the boat for the trip across southern Ontario through the Trent-Severn Waterway.

CHAPTER EIGHT

THE TRENT-SEVERN WATERWAY AND THE ST. LAWRENCE RIVER

T HE TRENT-SEVERN CANAL crosses southern Ontario, Canada, to provide a navigable link between Georgian Bay and Lake Ontario. Thirty-three miles of canals and 45 locks link together a natural series of lakes and rivers to form the 240-mile-long waterway. It opened in 1920 as a commercial shipping passage, but today, pleasure vessels have exclusive use of the waterway and the system is managed for recreational boating as a Heritage Canal by Parks Canada.

There is a flat fee to be paid for transiting the waterway, good for only five days. That five-day time limit presented me with a tight schedule. Each day, I would have to pass through nine locks and travel 50 miles.

The first lock at Port Severn was an easy lift of 14 feet up to the impounded waters of the Severn River. It was late in the day. I had been under way since before dawn and the weather had turned hot.

I was tired and dirty and in a hurry to make my daily quota of locks before they closed. Just above that first lock, the engine began to run wild and scream. I was able to row the boat to the shore where a quick investigation showed that the shear pin was the problem. Normally, a shear pin breaks when the propeller hits something. I had hit nothing; this pin had just disintegrated in its little slot.

I jumped overboard with pliers and wrenches, squatted down in belly-deep water, and made the repair. Above me on the river bank, two couples were seated around a linen-covered table enjoying a picnic. One of the men, about my age, sat there in a lawn chair observing me as I crouched in the water, muddy and grease-covered from neck to toes and fumbling for lost tools in the muck of the bottom. He was sipping a drink from a tall, thin-stemmed wine glass and he was dressed in an immaculate white linen suit, white shoes and a wide-brimmed Panama hat. In that moment, I wanted to trade places with him. In that moment, I wanted to say, "Enough of this god-damned voyage. Go home and be with Her; she who is always neat and clean, and picnic with her on a white, linen-covered picnic table beside some quiet gentle stream."

But that was only a passing thought. I revived my spirits with a dirty breakfast coffee cup of rum, started the engine, and cruised up the gentle Severn to the huge marine railway lift at the place called Big Chute. I anchored below the railway to observe how it worked before committing myself to the large, track-carried platform that lifts boats over the 58-foot high dam. It bears describing.

The carriage itself is 80 feet long and three storeys high. In operation, the carriage — like a huge, square bathtub — is submerged and boats simply float over to be cradled by an ingenious system of slings and supports. Then the carriage is pulled upward on tracks, the water drains out and boats make the trip dry. This "dry" portage — much more complicated than a conventional lock — was designed to keep the parasitic lamprey eel from migrating upstream.

My first overnight stop on the Trent-Severn was at the little community of Orillia on Lake Couchiching where I tied up to a dock in the city park. I remember the place and the night not because of anything special but because it was so ordinary. Shortly after dark a group of teenagers came down to the dock to swim. The girls carried large, over-the-shoulder bags that contained their hair dryers and combs. They asked me to keep their equipment on the boat while they swam. Because of that small event, on a warm evening with a bunch of small-town kids on a swimming party, I — so many miles from home — was less the stranger in a strange town.

Notes from the Log:
Red spots dot the white inside walls of the cabin, each the blood mark of one mosquito out of the dozens I have killed tonight. A rather gory decorating motif but I have to get rid of them before I can sleep.

Lake Simcoe, 19 miles long and 16 miles wide, was the last "dread" on my list of the dreaded unknowns. The Small Craft Guide carried this warning:

Caution — Sudden storms are frequent on Lake Simcoe and every care and seamanlike precaution should be observed when navigating the lake, especially in small craft.

The guidebook also mentioned that winds up to 25 miles an hour occurred in all months of the year and that such winds, blowing up the long axis of the lake, could kick up waves five and six feet high. As usual, I contemplated the worst and hoped for the best as I started out across Lake Simcoe. The lake was a mill pond, not a breath or a ripple, and I crossed it and tied up behind a breakwater that protected the lock at the mouth of the Talbot River. As I was waiting for the lock to open, a sudden, fierce wind blew in from the lake, uprooted trees and filled the air with swirling twigs and leaves. By only minutes I had escaped a summer thunderstorm that would have caught me in the open lake and probably swamped the boat.

The next ten miles of the waterway are controlled by five locks. These locks — and all the locks in the system — are controlled by hand-operated machinery that opens and closes the massive wooden gates of each lock. Each lock is surrounded by park-like grounds and gardens. Attendants, both men and women, wear the uniform of Parks Canada. They were consistently polite as they hand-cranked each of the locks I passed through, always greeting me with a friendly welcome and bidding me a "good luck" farewell.

The huge Kirkfield Hydraulic Lock carried me to the summit of the Trent-Severn Waterway, 840 feet above sea level. I thought the lock an engineering marvel. It consists of two side-by-side cantilevered chambers, each 140 feet long by 33 feet wide. For a boat to be lifted, it enters the water-filled lower chamber. The upper chamber is then flooded with water of a volume heavier than the boats and the water in the lower chamber. The heavy chamber slides down a track and its descending weight lifts the lower chamber. The mechanism requires massive supports of steel and concrete to lift 1,700 tons of water 50 feet in a seemingly effortless operation.

That night, I tied up to a tree on the wooded shore of Lake Balsam. I had climbed to the top of the Trent-Severn and I was in a celebratory mood. Behind me was the long route that led back down the Trent-Severn, across Georgian Bay to Mackinac Island, to Chicago, down the Illinois and the Mississippi to the mouth of the Missouri. Ahead of me lay the downslope of the Trent-Severn and the St. Lawrence to the Atlantic. Within the two routes, diverging as they did from my anchorage on Lake Balsam, were hundreds of miles of gleaming water reaching out across the land east, west and south. As a water traveler, I was able to comprehend that water-laced land like an old *voyageur.* Rivers and lakes told me where places were, where I was, and how to get where I wanted to go. A map of waters, not on paper, but visualized in my mind.

At Lake Balsam, I could tell by my feelings that the voyage — though it had many miles to go — was approaching its end. Could tell because I was already becoming nostalgic for places I had been. Much of the voyage had been squandered in grumbling and for many hours and miles I could give no account. Now, I wanted my mind and eyes to become like a movie camera, to record and keep all the impressions of the last miles so that, later, I could think back and say, "Yes, I remember that night on Lake Balsam, remember the storm that came in from the southeast, remember that my boat was a speck of light at the edge of that dark lake, held there by a rope tied to a tree, as I lay in my bunk listening to a Segovia concert, and I want to remember that I was there."

And Glen Ross, where I spent my last night on the Trent-Severn, I remember. It seemed a lonely little place: 15 houses and an abandoned store with fading signs advertising Coke, worms and hamburgers. A young girl rode her bike down to the canal bank and sat there, alone, just staring at the water. What, I wondered, does she think about as she looks at the river slowly moving downstream to the outside world? Does she come here every night by herself to rendezvous with her dreams? Will she marry and never leave this place by the canal? After a while, she got back on her bike and rode away, leaving me to wonder where she was going and what she would do when she got there.

An elderly woman came down to the boat and introduced herself as Mrs. Borris. She asked me about the boat. I told her I had built it. She said her husband was building a boat.

"You should see it," she said.

She left but within an hour returned with her husband.

"Come up to the house for dinner," he said. "I'd like you to look at my boat. I need some advice."

While Mrs. Borris prepared dinner, Mr. Borris and I examined the boat.

It was a derelict he had salvaged from the lake. I made a few suggestions. He seemed encouraged, and then we sat down for dinner. Their son was the subject of the dinner conversation. He was, they told me, a Hollywood screen writer. Proudly, they showed me the scrapbook of his press clippings that featured some of the major films he had worked on. Every winter, the Borrises go to southern California to visit their famous son.

In rapid succession, the final six locks of the Trent-Severn brought me down to the city of Trenton on the last day of my transit permit. At Trenton, I bought 30 gallons of gas and a box of groceries and the next morning, before dawn, I headed eastward through the Bay of Quinte in the far, upper northeastern corner of Lake Ontario.

I have vivid memories of that bright, moonlit morning before dawn as I worked my way along the shore of the Bay of Quinte. The black night and the moonlight made the shoreline stand out as a hard, ink-black silhouette. The water was a mirror of silver. I was alone on the bay, and I felt far away from everything, from everyone: a wonderful aloneness of myself, spinning off the miles of a dark shore, watching for the night to become dawn. I closed my eyes and, for a few seconds, slept. The boat ran on as though it knew where to go. When I wakened with a sudden start, it was to the reality of an old dream: myself, in a boat, traveling across the continent. Alone.

And with the dawn, I came to the old city of Kingston, Ontario. Street sweepers and garbage trucks were making their rounds and early morning workers were heading to shops and offices. I found a restaurant packed with office workers and listened in on conversations of office gossip. But I, the traveler, was a foreigner in the go-to-work routine of a city. I had arrived as a stranger out of the dawn and before the city would become fully awake, I would be traveling down another river, the St. Lawrence.

I entered the St. Lawrence where it spills out of Lake Ontario and through the scenic area of the Thousand Islands, but the beauty of the islands was wasted on me because I was in a hurry. She was going to meet me in Montreal, six locks and 250 miles down the river. She was to arrive there on June 16 and would wait for me. I was determined to get there first and surprise her and so, with a kind of bravado bordering on carelessness, I traveled down the wide St. Lawrence, argued my way through its locks and ignored channel markers as I cut across the bends of the river to save time. The weather was clear and I traveled with a wonderful sense of energy through the long, sun-filled hours as I hurried eastward through those last days of spring becoming summer.

One morning I stopped long enough to visit the restored farming settlement of Upper Canada Village. I tied the boat to a tree, climbed up the river bank and walked along a dirt road past plowed fields. Chickens scratched in the dust, geese raised their long necks and hissed at my passage, and cattle eyed me from the enclosures of their log fences. All the old farming equipment — shovels, long-handled rakes, a blacksmith's forge, wagons and plows — seemed left only yesterday by people of a different time. There was no one about the place, no cars, radios, stores or signs. Just a peaceful morning, as any day might have begun in the 18th-century time of a Canadian farm.

By contrast, a few hours later I went through the modern engineering marvel of the huge Eisenhower Lock, 80 feet wide by 730 feet long. It was the first of the locks on the US-Canada St. Lawrence Seaway. I took a picture of *Gander* in that lock. It shows the boat dwarfed beneath the high bow of an ocean freighter that went through the lock with me. I sat beneath the towering ship, thinking of all the things that could go wrong when the lock opened. What if my engine won't start? Does the ship's pilot know I am here? Will he run over me? Nothing went wrong. I got out of the lock as fast as I could when it opened, ran downriver for a half mile and hid behind a point until the ship passed.

Below Snell Lock, the St. Lawrence widens into Lac Saint Francois, 25 miles long and five miles wide. Halfway down the lake, a strong wind blew in from dead ahead and waves made up right behind it. Far down the lake I saw the white, onion-shaped dome of a church at a place the chart identified as St. Anicet. It became an object to steer toward, a place of shelter on a lake becoming rough.

I rounded the point on which the church stood and headed for a small dock in the lee of the point. It was marked private but it was the only dock in the cove. I tied the boat to the pier and walked up a short path to a house that overlooked the cove. A man and a woman were cleaning fish at an outside table. I asked permission to stay the night. They spoke only French, but I was able to understand that I could stay. I offered to pay but they declined the offer.

I walked around the quiet, tree-shaded streets of St. Anicet. At the small community store, I bought a large bottle of red wine and the grocer insisted on giving me a large loaf of freshly baked bread to go with it. I returned to the boat and invited the couple aboard for a glass of wine. They brought with them, as a gift, five pounds of freshly caught perch fillets.

The next morning the sun rose in a red-streaked sky. There was no wind and the lake was mirror calm. The onion-shaped tower, as I looked back at St. Anicet, was a column of soft pink. By a windstorm and a place of shelter, people and their gifts to a stranger — by these things I shall always remember the little community of St. Anicet.

And under that red morning sky, as I traveled alone down wide and empty Lac Saint Francois, 4,250 miles from home in the fourth summer of my voyage, I allowed myself the pleasure of contentment. This voyage, I thought to myself, I am doing here and now; I am where I am, and to this day and to this point, I have faithfully followed my compass of the dawn.

The next lock I entered, Beauharnois Lock, was operated by French-speaking Canadians. The previous three locks had been operated by Americans, and I had sailed right through them without any problems. At this lock, I went through the routine entry procedures, tied my mooring lines, and expected to be passed through the lock. An excitable French-speaking attendant began shouting at me but I could not understand what I was doing that was wrong. He disappeared and then returned with an English-speaking attendant. The problem, he explained to me, was that regulations forbade any boat to transit the lock with only one person aboard. He handed me down a book of regulations.

"Read the rules, read the rules," he shouted at me.

I did and they specifically stated that each boat was to be secured to the lock wall with a line fore and aft and that each line was to be tended at all times by a competent crew member. Two lines, two people — they had me on the regulations, but after all the locks I had transited, I figured myself sufficiently experienced to handle my boat alone. I explained all of that to the attendant but it did not impress him.

"Here," he insisted, "you must have two aboard to go through and that is the rule."

It was mid-morning. There were two more Canadian locks to go through before I would reach Montreal. The plane with *Her* aboard was going to arrive that afternoon and *I* was going to be there to meet it. The boat was halfway through the length of the lock; the upstream gate had closed behind me. Arguing with that excited lock attendant, I knew, would get me nowhere. So I sat down.

"If you won't let me through, then you will have to tow me out," I said.

This caused quite a disturbance, long lectures in both French and English as I continued to sit on the boat, ignoring them. Then they walked away. Ten minutes went by and they returned to tell me that I had been reported to the authorities and the authorities had said rules were rules: two crewmen to each boat. I shrugged my shoulders and remained seated. The two men disappeared again. Another ten minutes went by before they again returned, this time to order the attendant to lock me through. There were two remaining locks that I had to pass through, both of them operated by French-speaking attendants. Would the scene be repeated, I wondered?

It was not. Someone had phoned ahead to clear my way but I still received a lecture on the rules at each of the two passages. But I got through, one man, one boat, to the open St. Lawrence at Montreal.

And by 20 minutes, I beat *Her* to the airport — 32 days and 1,664 miles north and east from St. Louis.

CHAPTER NINE

DOWN TO THE ATLANTIC

WE HAD A WONDERFUL time in Montreal, stayed at McGill University, walked and walked the city streets and then rented a car and drove to Quebec City. But at the end of the week, I was anxious to get under way again. The next leg of the voyage would take me down the St. Lawrence, up the Richelieu River to Lake Champlain, then down the Hudson River to New York.

I said to her, "The Richelieu is supposed to be very pretty, very French, I am told. You must see it with me."

I tempted her with the prospect of two leisurely days on the river, stopping at little shoreside French restaurants for lunch and perhaps an overnight stay at an old inn.

She agreed to a night and two days.

It was uncomfortably warm on the Sunday morning as we left Montreal, the kind of muggy weather I knew preceded rain. Turning into the Richelieu, I was locked in a solid line of boats going upstream against another line coming downstream. These were big, fast boats, all passing us or coming at us, with their spreading wakes making an intersecting V of steep, quick wave furrows. There was no angle, no course I could steer to avoid these wakes and *Gander*, assaulted from every direction, leaped and jumped like a wild thing. I started looking for a cove, a dock, anyplace that would get us out of the concentrated, speed-mad boat traffic.

Odd thing about the lower Richelieu; there are no such places. The river runs straight and narrow without any breaks along its well-populated shore. Lunch time passed; no French restaurant, no restaurant of any kind.

"You will get out of the heavy traffic above the St. Ours Lock," the operator of a slower boat told me. "But you will have to hurry because it closes early."

We reached the lock five minutes after closing time.

"You can be the first boat through in the morning," the lock attendant told me as he locked his gatehouse and drove away. I tied the boat to a stone wall, then we went ashore looking for a restaurant. It had started to rain.

"There is a restaurant off the road about a mile back," a man told us. He said he would drive us part way there. He let us out at an intersection.

"Only a little way down the road," he said, and drove off.

We started walking. And walking. It was raining harder. We found the restaurant. It was closed. We walked back to the boat, walked as fast as we could because the sky was becoming ominously black. The storm broke just before we got to the boat and in seconds, we were drenched to the skin.

Back aboard, I put up the cockpit rain cover. She went into the cabin to dry her hair and change her clothes. The cabin was swarming with mosquitoes and it was impossible to kill them all. Though it was still warm, she put on a long-sleeved, high-neck sweater, long pants and my watch cap pulled down over her ears to protect herself from their bites. For dinner, we shared a can of cold salmon and sat huddled under the rain covering, watching the lightning flash and then waiting for the crash of thunder.

"Not exactly what I had planned," I said to her as later we lay in bed, me nearly naked in the warm cabin, she covered from head to toe by a wool blanket to ward off the mosquitoes.

In the morning, the weather had cleared. I went ashore and picked a bouquet of wildflowers for her and placed them in a vase on the galley drain-board. I then placed the bucket — *Gander* was not equipped with a toilet — in the cabin and left her to her privacy. When I returned, I lit the gas stove to make coffee and, as I turned away from the stove, I tipped over the vase of flowers and they fell into the flame of the lighted stove. Quickly I jumped to pull the flowers out of the flames and as I did so, I tipped over the bucket. Then I just sat down. I had hoped for so much on this little cruise and nothing had gone right.

Gently, she laid a hand on my arm.

"Please," she said, laughter in her eyes, "don't try so hard. Just let it be like it is when you're here by yourself. That's what I came to see and I haven't been disappointed."

We were the first boat through the lock in the morning and by noon, we were climbing the staircase of the nine consecutive locks at Chambly. At the top of the locks, there was a restaurant. It was open and the promised lunch, though not French, was served on a little terrace overlooking the river. Then, by bus, she returned to Montreal and I headed south, lonely as I had never been anywhere along the voyage.

That night, tied to a tree at Saint Jean sur Richelieu, I wanted to spend all my money for a 200-mile cab ride that would take me back to Montreal to see her again. Instead, I sat in the boat and by myself drank the bottle of red wine that was to have been served at our picnic stops on the Richelieu.

Lake Champlain, 110 miles long, is entered from the north on the Richelieu River and from the south by the 12 locks of the Champlain Canal which connect the lake to the Hudson River.

I had mixed emotions as I came up the Richelieu and reentered the United States at Rouses Point. My "other life" with my wife, and our home back in Portland, had been recalled by her bits of news about friends and relatives. It seemed so distant, a part of my life I had nearly forgotten. Her presence for two days in the simple and primitive conditions on the boat reminded me how simple and primitive my voyaging life had become. This outlook, this way of living, was what the voyage had demanded, was what the hard, tough miles had taught me.

Alive and alone, intensely so, ecstatically so at times, had been my days on a small boat throughout the long voyage. I knew that when I returned home there would be no place in ordinary living for dirt and grime and mud and wind and the kind of Spartan aloneness that wants nothing except the space and distance and time of the long-distance voyage. In less than 300 miles, a few months short of my 60th birthday, my journey would end. What then? I liked who I was, what I had become and in that lay the true cost of the voyage: I would have liked it to continue on. Forever, perhaps.

In Burlington, Vermont, where I stayed for three days, I hung a "For Sale" sign on the boat. The voyage was coming to an end and it was something that, sadly, had to be done because the boat was not worth the price of transporting it back across the continent. The sign caught the attention of a local newspaper reporter and his story of my trip brought dozens of people down to the dock where *Gander* lay. No one the bought the boat, but many dreams were told to me, along with complaints about jobs and families that prevented such dreams from becoming reality.

I left Burlington and ran down the length of Lake Champlain following my old road map, very happy that the voyage-worn *Gander* was still mine. Twin mountain ranges run the length of the lake: the Adirondacks of New York State to the west, the Green Mountains of Vermont to the east. It is all very pretty, very neat, and I was dressed for my trip through this very civilized lake in my dress-up blue blazer and white pants. They were stained and wrinkled but the best I could do to present a "yachty" appearance as I passed the settled, genteel shoreline of Lake Champlain with its large summer homes and rolling acres of green lawns.

That night, I anchored beneath the frowning crest of Crown Point and the warm, summer air carried with it the smell of a paper mill. The next day I joined a group of tourists for a tour through the massive fortifications of Fort Ticonderoga, a stronghold of the American Revolution. Like a diver coming slowly up through deep water to condition his body to a change in pressure, I was slowly reentering the world of people and the land.

Lake Champlain came to an end in long, finger-like leads and shallow marshes. The road map was sketchy on detail but ahead of me I saw what I was looking for: a low gap in the hills that permitted a water passage from the lake to the Hudson River. The town of Whitehall, New York, lies in that gap and it fronts Lock Number 12 at the northern end of the Champlain Canal.

From Whitehall, I called ahead to New York and talked to my youngest daughter, Phoebe. Divorce had formed barriers of time and distance between us. She was a child when the divorce occurred. Since then, she had graduated from Vassar College and was a young professional woman working in New York. We had seen each other over the years, but never long enough and never often enough to reassemble a close father-daughter relationship.

"Someday," I had told her, "someday I'll be coming your way in my boat and we will travel down the Hudson together." Someday had been a long time in coming, but she agreed to meet me the next day in Albany, New York.

My last night out, alone, was in Schuylerville, New York. I tied up at the bottom of Lock Number 5 and walked along a dirt road leading to the town. I had visited many places like Schuylerville: semi-rural communities that somehow lived on long after they had any economic reason to do so. But Schuylerville seemed to be a particularly down-and-out place, a town that reflected many of the growing ills of rural America.

The town was a pizza parlor, a video store, a mini-market and a gas station — plastic and neon-lit enterprises that seemed to serve only the pleasures of the town's teenage and young adult population. During my evening there, I watched these young people drive from one end of the town to the other and then back again in what seemed to me to be a pathetically small orbit of frenzied, noisy and pointless motion.

I felt a sense of fury when, as a gang, they passed me, an older man walking their street, and shouted curses and obscenities at me.

And, by contrast, I felt a sense of sadness when, as individual kids, they were shy and reluctant to speak to me in my attempt at a restaurant conversation.

And what would I have told them, had any one of them been interested in what I had to say? Something about the voyage, something about the man who was passing through their town because he was being true to an old dream of his youth. I would have told them that they, too, should dare to dream and then make their lives bear witness to those dreams. I would have told them that it was not money nor skill nor knowledge that had carried me across the continent, only the sense of what I thought I could do. On nothing more tangible than that, I would have said, do all voyages begin.

Last note in the Log:
Entered the last river today, the Hudson. It flows to the Atlantic.

Phoebe met me at the Albany Yacht Club across the Hudson from Albany. Her enthusiasm for the voyage with me was written all over her face in a wide, eager smile. I hoped — Lord, how I hoped — that she would not be disappointed. I had a lot resting on our trip together: the finding of a lost daughter. During the next few days, in the closeness of a very small boat, we spanned the years of separation with small adventures, memories and laughs as we traveled down the wide Hudson.

We walked the streets of Kingston in a driving rainstorm and then stopped at Poughkeepsie, the site of her alma mater. She showed me around the campus, pointing out her classrooms to share with me a time of her life I had never known. While there, we were invited for dinner and a day sail on the famous Hudson River sloop *Clearwater*, built by singer Pete Seeger to initiate a clean-up of the river. Phoebe immediately found friends among the enthusiastic and articulate crew of young people. She got to "show off her dad" to these people who saw me as an old but interesting character they respected because of my trans-continental voyage.

Peekskill, New York, was the last night of the voyage. The next day we ran the last few miles of the Hudson, with Phoebe using a road map to pilot me through the busy harbor of New York. We turned into the Harlem River and then went down the East River, passing beneath the Brooklyn Bridge and by the United Nations Building. At the tip of Manhattan Island, the continent ended and so did the trip. There, Phoebe took charge and showed me something of her city, then left me at the boat dock at the South Street Seaport Maritime Museum.

I was a guest of the museum for three days. During that time, the staff did everything possible to help me sell the boat. No buyers showed up so I decided that I would go back up the river and give the boat to the *Clearwater* people to sell for the support of their cause. Halfway along the Hudson River side of Manhattan Island, I came to the West 79th Street Boat Basin, noticed an interesting collection of boats, and turned in. The "For Sale" sign was still hanging on the boat.

A small group of young people formed around the boat as I introduced myself. One young man asked if he could look inside. After a half-hour of discussion, he agreed to buy it. It was an interesting sale. He went uptown to his money machine, came back with $1,000 in cash and I wrote out a title to the boat on a brown paper bag. The next day, I put the engine, books, charts and my notes in a wooden box, called a delivery service to ship it to Portland and boarded a plane for home.

As I flew westward at 32,000 feet back over the route I had traveled, the land below sped past like a fast-moving film running backwards. It took only six hours to cover the distance that had taken me the summers of four years. Below, I could see the occasional glint of a river, the shining expanse of a distant lake, and valleys of green that hid wandering streams. There, along those waters, I had traveled from west to east across the continent on a voyage that had included 15 US states, two Canadian provinces, 11 rivers, 43 lakes, 89 navigation locks, and more than a hundred cities and towns, through sandbars and swamps and long days of heat, dust, wind and rain. Looking down through the plane window at the immense span of the continent, I thought it impossible that I had actually made that long voyage.

But I knew I had because I was carrying home proof: four years added to my life since the day when I started at the edge of the Pacific Ocean. And scars: the evidence of many small accidents on my hands and feet, and in my mind memories of people met and places loved and places cursed. Then the plane landed. She met me for a joyous homecoming. The memento of the small rock I had gathered from an obscure Missouri River beach was placed above my desk, and the voyage was a thing of the past. My Everest, climbed.

SECTION THREE

WOODEN BOATS, WESTERN WATERS

Chapter One

REACH OF TIDE

THAT TRIP ACROSS NORTH America spanned a huge geography of history, the explorations of rivers that preceded the American westward movement. Out of the interest in history the voyage created, I got a job with the Oregon Historical Society in Portland to coordinate the bicentennial celebration of Robert Gray's 1792 discovery of the Columbia River.

I was to assist the towns and communities of the lower river in the development of their historical resources. For such a job, I reasoned, a boat was essential as a means of getting to know the river and the histories of those towns along the tidewater reach of the Columbia. And so began three years of pleasant work on the river with a boat and the writing of a book, *Reach of Tide, Ring of History*, about the lower Columbia, the book that gave the name to the boat.

Reach of Tide was similar to the little bluff-bowed *Gander I* but much larger: 26 feet overall. That bluff bow allowed the boat to be beached on the many islands of the lower river, and its shallow draft let me negotiate the backwater sloughs. For three years and hundreds of miles, I traveled the river, talking to its old fishermen, trying to convince the leaders of little communities that they were an important part of the Columbia River's history and, as such, that they should take pride in who they were and what they had been. Out of this work small museums were formed, main streets spruced up, oral history programs developed and something of a pride of place generated in those river communities. This was the modest legacy of my time on the river in *Reach of Tide*.

There were no harrowing adventures on those river trips as there had been on the voyage across America, no long distances to cover, no heat or windstorms to hide from. Many of my voyages in *Reach of Tide* were to its namesake waters, the estuary of the lower Columbia, the place where river currents meet the tide, where fresh water mingles with salt. Weather sets the mood of the estuary: storm-swept, rain-washed, sun-drenched, foggy or overcast, with each mood reflected in colors of blue, green, silver and many shades of gray.

Reach of Tide.

Not one line but many define the perimeter of the estuarine shore, its borders contracting and expanding with the cycles of rising and falling water.

I could watch this line change as I straddled the shoreline at the river's edge, one foot on land, the other in the water. In moments, the line would change: on the flood tide, what had been land would become river; on the ebb, what had been river would become land. Across that changing line between water and earth, life had emerged from water to breathe air.

My voyages through the estuary discovered the connections that are its themes: connections I could feel and hear as I walked barefoot over sand or through squishy mud, dangled my feet from the edges of old docks, witnessed the dawn flight of geese, the poised, stiff-legged stance of the heron, the forest-framed stillness of the deer.

The constant companion of my river travels in *Reach of Tide* was a cat named Gray Bear. One day when I was building the boat, she wandered in from somewhere, crawled up in the bow and never left.

She got her name because when I held her, she would put her paws around my neck in a bear hug, so Gray Bear became her name. She was a great character, full of tricks and quirks. She frequently fell overboard and I would retrieve her from the water with a large fish-net. When I beached the boat on an island, Gray Bear would jump out, ecstatically dig numerous holes in the sand, and then go back aboard the boat to do her business in her sandbox. Whenever I docked, Gray Bear was first ashore for a grand tour of all the boats in the harbor — a hand-out here, a pet there, for her winning ways.

I loved that cat, and when she became painfully and terminally ill, I had the courage to have her put down. She died in my arms, bear hugging me. I made a box for her body, threw in one of my old pipes, a sailing jacket and a few of her rope-end toys, took her in the boat down to a river island we had visited together, and buried her.

Last note in the Log of *Reach of Tide*:
So home I go without Gray Bear. Wind and tide are running free to carry *Reach of Tide* to a new owner.

CHAPTER TWO

ROWING TO ASTORIA

WHEN MY JOB WITH the historical society ended, I was without a boat and ahead of me lay the doubtful plea- sures of retirement. My 70th birthday loomed and I felt grounded on the fast ebbing tide of time. I had everything: lovely wife, home, friends, reasonable financial security and good health. But I was becoming somewhat complacent and sometimes bored and it seemed that I was more and more looking backwards, recalling the life I had lived in the past instead of anticipating how I could live in the future.

The build-up of routines, the little moats of protecting opinions and prejudices I had gathered around me, were starting to wall me in. As were possessions: three-piece suits and neckties no longer necessary, books I would never read again, a huge photograph collection, old letters and family keepsakes. Downstairs, my workshop garage housed a cluttered assortment of left-over boat parts, old engines, dried paint cans and boxes of unsorted nails and screws. My life, I thought, had become a bit like that shop: a clutter of the superfluous. Travel, something I had always enjoyed, had come to mean crowded highways, look-alike strip malls, and soulless jet travel from airport to airport to visit exotic places of the world trampled by the Nike-clad feet of a thousand tourists. I was losing the battle in trying to accept the contentment of retirement. What I wanted was the *dis*contentment of an idea or a project, something that would give urgency and direction to time, a new challenge for muscle and mind. In the dory, I had gone as far north as I could; the three *Ganders* had carried me across the continent. Where and what now? I asked myself.

I found the seed of what I was looking for in a book written by the German climber Reinhold Messner who made a solo climb of Mount Everest. Wrote Messner: "Like a snail which carries its home on its back I carry my tent in my rucksack. I shall erect it, sleep in it and take it with me for the next night. I am equipped like a nomad."

Years ago, I did a lot of mountain climbing. What I remember most vividly about those years were my climbs in the Tetons of Wyoming, not the summits climbed but the days of just living high up in the mountains with only a light tent, a tiny stove and simple food. Wonderful were those days and nights up there on some protected ledge, totally reliant on nothing more than what I could carry on my back, self-contained in storm and sun, moving from place to place as desire and inclination prompted. It was a time of living with only the essentials: a mountain nomad like Messner.

I converted this philosophy of simplicity to water travel by building a rowboat and began to condition myself for a hundred-mile row to Astoria to celebrate my 70th birthday.

Rowing Notes:
This is day three in my attempt to turn a 69-year-old, semi-atrophied body into a muscular machine for rowing; back like a flexible, loaded spring, piston-like arms to pull the oars, and legs like hinges to push and pull me back and forth on the sliding rowing seat.

146

Today, sitting on the rowing seat and less than a mile from the dock, my butt hurts with the most pressing pain. It feels as though I am attached to the boat seat by two swollen boils on my buns, festering abscesses that scream out in such pain that I wonder if my body will ever become conditioned to the demands of long-distance rowing.

Each day for five days after I finished building the boat, I set for myself a more distant goal, with a thicker pillow beneath my rear end. I gave full attention to the motion of my arms, the placement of my feet and the angle and reach of the oars. On the fifth morning, I reached a condition of reasonable harmony between these subtle but critical rowing dimensions: rear end comfortably padded, feet positioned at an easy angle, oar handles just touching as they crossed each other with each stroke. On that day, I crossed what an experienced rower told me was the threshold of long-distance rowing.

"Go for an hour," he said, "and you can go forever."

He didn't say miles, he said time, because time — timing — is the essence of rowing. Properly orchestrated, like a string trio, the rowing triad of body, boat and oars can approach something rarely obtainable: a perfection of motion in the timing of strokes and pauses and rests.

Such a simple thing, a rowing boat; an ancient mechanism to move a person through water. Its predecessors were first a crude pole and a raft, later a paddle and a canoe, and then a boat with twin oars to replace pole and paddle. And some things, like breathing, living, dying, and the seasons — along with rowing — do not change over the centuries. Metal and plastics have made the rowing boat of today a strong and light foundation for the oars but what sticks out, what enters water to find substance to push against, is still two sticks with paddles at their outer ends. Early man would find few things of this century familiar to him, but the rowboat he would recognize as a familiar object. And probably know how to make it go.

When I rowed a hundred miles down the Columbia River to Astoria, my view was backwards — as it is for all rowers — and the future was a fleeting glance over my shoulder, peripheral impressions of what lay ahead. What I could see for most of the time was not where I was going but where I had been and with each stroke of the oars, the scene behind me receded further into a past of time and distance.

Stroke, pause and pull. The oars would dip, lift from the water as glistening blades, balance for a second in the air, and then disappear under the surface of the river. As they rose from the water at the completion of a stroke, they left behind little rippled rings of water, the circled waterprints of my passage.

The hours would pass — stroke, pause and pull — at a leisurely pace of 20 strokes to the minute, 1200 to the hour. Each stroke moved the boat ahead about ten feet. Astoria, my mind calculated, was 520,000 feet and 52,000 strokes away. I tried not to count, to row rhythmically, efficiently and gracefully, to think of myself as some kind of water animal with oars the outward extensions of my body. But rowing was the occupation of my body, not my mind.

The rowboat, on the way to Astoria.

That dimension of me was free to float, to wander through meditations and memories that would block out the pain and fatigue and monotony of the rowing strokes. With discipline, I was able to release my mind from my body by making it reach out for the bits and pieces of half-formed ideas that would flit through my head like moths. Out of some of these thoughts, I could make stories and in these stories, I was someone else in some other place telling me a story.

In my boat, future became past as the shoreline unrolled before and behind me, my course a reflection of its curves and bends. By the liquid sculpturing of rain, flood and tide, the contours of that shoreline had been drawn; by the seasons, weather and the time of day, its moods and colors had been etched. It was a marginal wilderness, a flood plain of moist ground, swamps, trees and brush uninhabitable by anything that cannot adapt to the changing levels of high and low water, current and mud. A place of no use for the purposes of man — the exclusive realm of the water's edge.

Tiny goslings, like feathered ping-pong balls, skittered for shelter at my approach, their nervous parents honking them to safety. Herons stood still in their watchful stances on arching snags and a muskrat squinted at me in the bright sun before disappearing in the leaf carpet beneath the wall of brush. To follow this shoreline, to quietly observe those river creatures, for those things I built this boat and chose to power it with arms and noiseless oars.

Stroke, pause and pull.

Passing beneath a bridge, I looked up to see and hear cars speeding across the bridge, 50, 60 miles an hour to my three to four on the river. Time — that critical dimension within which we live — sent those cars speeding across that bridge, to get somewhere in the least possible time as their drivers traveled unseeing miles, windows rolled up, radio on or cellular phone in hand, oblivious to the river below. I, too, have been the victim of the obsession to save time, to go fast, to get someplace quickly. But my perspective was different on the river looking up at the freeway, moving at a rate of speed only a little faster than walking. I wanted to enjoy where I was going, and to know where I had been. Concentration, attention, a sense of traveling that involves full participation of body and mind is what was produced by that rowing journey. Time, the journey had, that most precious of all things, that dimension that is life itself.

And with time, my intimacy with the river was magnified and enlarged. Each tree was seen as a single tree, the composite wholeness of trunk, branches and leafy crown. I observed the infinite variety and shape of each passing twig and floating bit of wood. Out on the river, I saw each day begin as the sun moved up from the horizon of dark to dawn, its bright, warming glow spreading light across the calm river which slowly became ruffled as the morning wind dragged its skirts across the water. I watched the rain that dappled the river with millions of little ringed circles, each capped by a bubble-dome where the drop hit the river. I rowed through a skin of circles, each one the concluding instant in the life of a raindrop blown in from the sea to fall into the river and return again to the sea.

And with such Zen-like thoughts, I traveled a hundred miles down the Columbia in three days, island-camping along the way like a water nomad. Out of rowing, flab had turned to muscle, and my mind was revitalized. If at 70 I could row a hundred miles, then I figured I could also return to the sea.

CHAPTER THREE

A YAWL CALLED *SPRAY*

T O RETURN TO THE sea, my wife and I moved to Vancouver,
British Columbia, and I went looking for a boat to travel
that vast inland sea lying between the BC mainland and
Vancouver Island.

"Come down to Winslow," said a Bainbridge Island yacht-broker
friend of mine. "There is a boat here that might interest you. It's a
replica of Slocum's boat, the *Spray*. It's for sale cheap but it needs
some work."

A hulk cheap but ready to sink, I thought, wanting to still an
excited heart, but the next day I drove down to Bainbridge Island
just to take a look.

"The boat has been for sale for two years and the owner has to
leave the country," the broker advised me when I got to Winslow.
"Make him any kind of an offer and he'll probably accept it." He
loaned me his skiff to row out to where the boat was anchored in
the harbor.

Scattered about were the clean, sleek-lined, factory-produced yachts, varnished rails and stainless steel bright in the sunlight, an anchored flotilla worth hundreds of thousands of dollars. Then, on the far edge of the fleet I saw it: the long sheer, bluff bow, square stern, poking bowsprit and wooden masts of an unmistakable *Spray*, taken from the lines of the boat in which Joshua Slocum made his famous solo circumnavigation of the world more than a century ago.

The boat looked very much alone and neglected with a painted "For Sale" sign dangling over its side. Loose ropes swung in the rigging, their frazzled ends swaying in the gentle wind. Green was the color of the boat, the green of a moss coating that covered the cabin tops, oozed down the cabin sides and spread across the decks as slime. But what a marvelous hull — broad beamed, low slung amidships but lifting along the line of the bulwarks to a high, proud bow. Twice, I rowed around the boat, my eyes following the complex tracery of rigging leading from the deck to the top of the wooden mast.

I was almost reluctant to step aboard, to break the magic that clung to this boat in spite of its run-down appearance. "Leave it be, keep the dream and spare yourself a lot of work," my better sense told me. I knew what to expect; I had examined many boats for sale "cheap": black, oily water in the bilge; a grease-covered, useless engine webbed by frayed electrical wires; sodden mattresses in the dark corners of bunks; dirty pots and pans, shelves with swollen boxes of crackers and rusty tins of beans. Everything saying abandoned, left, as in so many old boats because of unpaid bills, divorce, death: the boat that was left behind at the end of a broken dream. But then — always the optimist — maybe this one, this replica of Slocum's old boat, could be fixed up to sail again. It was worth a peek below.

I tied the rowboat to the rail and climbed aboard, unlocked the hatch and stepped below. Shafts of sunlight entering the cabin through brass-ringed portholes reflected off the varnished surfaces of the cabin walls, giving to the patterned ceiling of curved, dark beams a warm under-glow. Bookshelves lined one wall of the cabin, an immaculate stainless-steel sink was tucked under the cupboards that ran along the other side. Forward, a large cabin with a clean, double bunk was lit by an overhead skylight. Forward of that, two bunks lay in the V of the bows, their mattresses covered with neat coils of rope, and above them blocks hung from hooks. I lifted the lid off the engine box. Inside was a diesel engine, brand new, spotless.

I was probably not breathing as I trod softly through that snuggery of brass and varnished wood, the touch of my hands on cabin walls, counters, beams and ceiling telling me what my eyes could not believe — that this boat could be mine.

And so it became with the signing of my name on a piece of paper; the *Northern Spray* — overall length 55 feet, beam 15 feet, draft 5 feet, weight 36,000 pounds — was now my boat. I would go looking no more. I had bought not only a boat but a legend: the legend of Joshua Slocum and the famous yawl *Spray*.

In 1892, Joshua Slocum was a ship captain without a ship to command. His career had been in sailing ships but the era of wind ships was over and steam commanded the sea.

"As for a ship to command," he wrote in his book *Sailing Alone Around the World*, "there were not enough ships to go round. Nearly all our tall vessels had been cut down for coal barges, and were being ignominiously towed by the nose from port to port, while many worthy captains addressed themselves to Sailors Snug Harbor."

Slocum was not yet ready for the Sailors Snug Harbor but what, he asked, "was there for an old sailor to do?" For two years he had been largely unemployed in and around Boston. Then, while walking the Boston docks in 1892, he met an old acquaintance who said, "Come to Fairhaven and I'll give you a ship." The friend advised Slocum that "she wants some repairs."

The boat given to Slocum was the hulk of a century-old oyster boat named *Spray*. But more than some "fixing," was needed. The boat had to be rebuilt from the keel up at a cost for Slocum of $553.62. For 13 months he worked on the boat in Fairhaven and, with his own hands fashioned every timber and plank and the sails and rigging that went into the making of his new boat.

"The *Spray* changed her being so gradually," wrote Slocum, "that it was hard to say at what point the old died or the new took birth." In the process of rebuilding the boat, Slocum also rebuilt his life. His question of what was there for an old sailor to do was answered with his decision to sail single handed around the world. On the morning of April 24, 1895, he sailed out of Boston to begin his three-year, 46,000-mile solo voyage around the world.

Slocum's route carried him first across the Atlantic to Gibraltar, then back across the Atlantic and south along the South American coast. He made a stormy passage through Magellan Strait, then crossed the southern Pacific to Australia, passed that continent to the north, and crossed the Indian Ocean to the Cape of Good Hope. He sailed across the South Atlantic to South America, then north to the United States and ended the voyage in Fairhaven on July 3,1898.

In his book, Slocum included the plans and dimensions of his *Spray*. A technical analysis of the boat was made in 1909 by marine architect C. Andrade, Jr. "I attacked her," he wrote, "and she emerged from the ordeal a theoretically perfect boat." He concluded his analysis of *Spray*'s lines by stating that "not only an able boat, but a beautiful boat" because its form is "perfectly adapted to perform its allotted work."

I slept aboard the boat the night I bought *Northern Spray*. The next day, I rented a power washer and cleaned off the moss. With a friend, I sailed it to Vancouver and had it surveyed, something normally done before a person buys a boat. I just knew that *Northern Spray* was in good shape and the survey confirmed that hunch. Even so, a long list of things to do emerged as I became acquainted with the boat. The electrical system, though in good working order, was in a bit of tangle. Most of the running rigging needed replacing. I had the rainy weather of a Vancouver winter ahead of me: time to fix what needed fixing, time to become acquainted with my new boat.

A few papers aboard told the boat's history. It had been built in a cooperative boatyard in Sausalito, California, in 1980. Dudley Lewis, the builder, was a liberal political activist. He launched it

Northern Spray *at the Vancouver Maritime Museum, Vancouver, British Columbia.*

with the name *Hermanos y Hermanas* ("Brothers and Sisters") and used it to transport medical supplies to Nicaragua to aid the victims of the 1988 Contra war. Then he tried fishing, unsuccessfully, off the California coast. He sold the boat to the man from whom I bought it and this man sold it to me "cheap" because he was moving to Kenya in Africa to teach community woodworking.

I wrote Dudley a letter, telling him that I had bought the boat he had built and outlined some of the plans I had for its use. He wrote back, saying, "From your letter it sounds like the vessel has finally found a master worthy of her. As you probably know, she was built with massive 6" x 6" sawn cedar frames, glued and riveted with 3/8" iron tugboat spikes. Her planks, also of cedar, are riveted with copper rivets between the frames and 6" Scotch-cut copper spikes on the frames. She was built to last several lifetimes. She was a comfortable, heavy weather work boat that would self-steer as long as the wind blew steady."

I felt it my responsibility to keep what Dudley had built in good condition so that it would, indeed, "last several lifetimes." So *Northern Spray* became my sea school as I learned the skills of the shipwright, mechanic, painter, rigger and electrician. And as I worked with ropes, diesel engines, stoves, pumps, and electrical systems, I had just over my shoulder both old Slocum and Dudley, always reminding me of the old sailor's adage that "if a thing ain't done right, it's wrong."

What I quickly discovered, as I made a list of the things that had to be done aboard *Northern Spray,* was the inter-relatedness of all things on a big boat: a complicated assemblage of parts and pieces, that, though separate, contribute in their specialized ways to the overall performance of the boat. What I had to learn and understand was the function and linkage of these various systems.

Aloft is the sailing rig: the mast, shrouds, halyards, lazy jacks, and back stays. These wires and ropes each have a specific function and I had to learn how to use each of them in sailing the boat at night-time as well as in the day.

Below is the diesel engine, an intertwined connection of hoses, pipes, pulleys and belts. There is the battery, the source of light, the starter of the engine, the generator, the radio, the depth sounder, and the pumps. And then there are the pumps that carry water to the engine, to the sink and overboard from the toilet. Confusing and complicated, all these parts and systems, yet in each there is a kind of simplicity that responds to set laws of physics, efficiency and utility.

Rope, for example. It is a mechanism of geometry and physics, one of the oldest and simplest of man's inventions, something that emerged from the woven vines that man has used to make him master of the wind. The function of rope is simple: under tension, it connects opposing forces. I, pulling on a rope, transmit a force that overcomes gravity and friction.

The unique feature of soft, pliable rope is that it can carry force up from the deck to the block at the peak of the mast and then down to the deck. Its forces can go around corners and be multiplied with a block and tackle and — when not needed — it can lie in coiled repose until again called upon to transmit power from one place to another.

A job that had to be done was to hook the mainsail block to the top of the mast. Without it, the boat was incomplete, crippled and, in a way, so was I as a sailor because of my fear of going aloft to place it. The sensible thing for me to have done would be to hire some young, monkey-like rigger to do the job for me. But no, I could imagine old Slocum laughing at me because of my fear. "Get up there," he would say. "If you are afraid to go aloft, then you shouldn't own a sailing vessel."

And so with a friend hauling on the mainsail winch, I was lifted 40 feet up to the top of the mast. What surprised me was that I felt no fear. Not comfortable in the sling that bit into my crotch, but not afraid as I thought I would be. The absence of fear allowed me to relax my tight stomach muscles, let me concentrate on the delicate job of shackling the block to an eye on the mast. "Up a bit," I hollered down to the man working the winch below me. The sling tightened and my feet, wrapped around the mast, scraped against its wood as I was inched upward another foot. The eye was now just an arm's reach above me. The block, with its metal strap and shackle and its long dangling halyard, was heavy.

I paused and took a long breath and then waited another moment. I put the pin in my mouth and clenched it there in my teeth. Then, balancing the block in my right hand, I thrust my hand upward. I had only a few seconds before my arm would collapse, before my fingers would cramp. They had to feel their way, because I could not see what they were doing. In the last split seconds of my arm and hand strength, the block was in position. I took the shackle pin from my mouth and slowly carried it upwards in my left hand and gently pushed it into the shackle. The block for the mainsail was in place and *Northern Spray* was given its wings.

Were I 20 years younger, I would probably lift those wings and follow in the track of Slocum around the world. But now, at 72, just owning such a boat is satisfaction enough. I will again go a-voyaging. Slocum had the world to go around. I have the world of Vancouver Island and a thousand islands to circumnavigate. And there is still some time for me, a boat and the sea.

CHAPTER FOUR

REQUIEM FOR MY HEROES

I CLOSE THIS BOOK with the satisfaction that I have fulfilled most of my dreams. I write this not as a boast but as a tribute to those — named and nameless — who seeded them and kept them alive. What they taught me, what they showed me, how they inspired me, is something of a loan that had to be paid back by doing the best I could to follow in their wakes.

And so Wes Bush, captain of *Dubloon*, we didn't make it to Tahiti but I learned a lot about sailing from you. And now I hold my coastal skipper's certificate and command a small ship. Now, I too, am looking for a kid — the kind of kid you found in me when I crewed for you aboard *Dubloon* — to come aboard *Northern Spray* and learn how to sail a boat.

As for you, Joe, the recluse of Barkley Sound, I have not forgotten your admonition to "put something back." For ten years I taught adventure education programs at a university, taught young students how to climb and sail. In the process, they learned something about themselves and what they were capable of doing. Out of that role at the university, I went on to found the Northwest Outward Bound School, a program that brought the same learning experiences to thousands of other young people.

Another project of mine was the hundred-mile river wilderness kayak trail I developed during the years I spent working on the Columbia. *Northern Spray* is continuing that mission. With the Vancouver Maritime Museum, I lead cruises of environmental and historical interest through British Columbia waters. Thanks to you, Joe; it has been a pleasure to be able to put something back.

Some years ago, I met an Englishman named Michael Jeneid. Michael's specialties are ocean kayaking and rock climbing. His techniques were perfected during World War II when he taught British commandos to land in the surf and climb the cliffs behind the beach. He is also a poet, and the nighttime adventures of landing a small boat in the surf and cliff-climbing in the dark appealed to his poetic sense. Then one night his operation landed on the Normandy beaches and at the top of the cliff his men were all killed.

That finished Michael's career as a soldier-poet. After the war he took his kayak to the Great Barrier Reef of Australia, Cape Horn and other wild places of the earth where the ocean meets the shore in gigantic waves. When he wasn't kayaking, he was climbing because Michael felt that there was something within these two pursuits that was worthwhile, something of poetry and philosophy that would make death by gunfire at the top of a cliff unnecessary.

When I met Michael, he was teaching kayaking and climbing on an island off the Maine Coast. His courses had only two grades: pass or fail. His students were young, hard-core criminals referred to him by the New York Crime Commission. Somehow, a life-survival trip with Michael through the ocean in an open kayak or scrambling up a rock cliff was something that appealed to them, something they could do without the need of a gun. Afterwards, their lives and bodies having been committed to these highly dangerous endeavors, they found that just being alive was something of value.

Out of my conversations with Michael were born my political beliefs which, like his, are a simple reverence for life in all its forms and the environment in which it lives: the land, the sea, the tides, the wind and the rain.

Beyond these men are the ones I have never met, the ones I know only through their books. They are the soul of my on-board library, my companions of adversity. Not men I ever hoped to emulate — their adventures were outside my scale of doing — but men who showed me what could be accomplished by a man and a boat through dedication, endurance and courage.

Odd, I think, that a man my age still has his heroes. But I do and occasionally, in a tight spot of wind and sea, I call out their names as a way of calming my fears and ask, "What should I do?" They are there, answering me from out of their knowledge, their experience, and compassion.

"Stay calm," they say. "Look fear in the face and stare it down and then — you dummy — reef the mainsail!" Willingly, I accept their orders; they are my hero-captains. They would not think of themselves as heroes; the sea has made them too humble to wear this mantle. Who are they, these men who so often stand at the tiller with me? I name a few:

Slocum, of course; very demanding as to how I sail his boat, but always there to give me encouragement.

Harry Pidgeon is another. He was a restless farm boy, ran the Yukon River in an Indian-style canoe. In 1917 on the mudflats of Wilmington, California, he built a 34-foot boat known as a "Seabird" yawl. Twice he sailed around the world, then, coming ashore, he lived for 16 years aboard that boat. At age 75 he set out again for a second circumnavigation. Why is Pidgeon one of my heroes? Because he was a farm boy with no boat-building knowledge, no sea-faring skills, who taught himself how to build a boat, how to sail it and how to navigate. Pidgeon showed me that I could learn by doing and by doing, I have learned what I know. And by going around the world at 75, he showed me that old age is no excuse for not going to sea. "You can sail for one day, can't you? That's all it is — one day after another," he wrote.

And there are others:

Vito Dumas, west to east around Cape Horn — the opposite way for most sailing vessels — in the ketch *Lehg II*.

Bernard Moitessier, an entrant in the first round-the-world race, was miles ahead of his competitors when he rounded Cape Horn, but instead of finishing the race as a winner, he went on around the world again to sail in ten months 37,455 miles.

My hero turned role model was the crusty, pipe-smoking, sailor-mountaineer H. W. Tilman. British to his toes was this life-long adventurer, in style, demeanor and outlook. After spending over seven years exploring the Himalayas with his climbing companion, Eric Shipton, he was asked by Shipton if they could begin calling each other by their first names. Tilman's reply was, "Not just yet, Mr. Shipton."

He combined sailing with mountaineering and in his old pilot boat *Mischief*, he made sailing-mountaineering expeditions to Greenland, Iceland, Baffin Island and, lastly, Antarctica where he was lost at sea. Tilman is the man I most frequently call on when I am facing danger. I always know what his advice will be: "Let's light up a pipe, Mr. McKinney, and think this thing through."

There are others, a long list of men who share with me a love of the sea and a boat and lean toward the traditional way of things: caulked wooden planks, pine tar, woolen underwear, pipe smoke, tea and navy rum.

With them I can share this in accomplishment: that we had our dreams and, more than that, we have tried to live those dreams.

POSTSCRIPT

THIS WAS A MAN I met over in the Gulf Islands. Sometime during the night, he had silently come in and tied his boat to the next dock over from where I was moored. In the morning we became acquainted over a cup of coffee. I estimated his age as somewhere in the 70s. He was over six feet tall and his pants — cut off as a ragged cuff above the ankle — were held up by a single suspender crossing his chest. He walked around barefooted.

His boat was an old ship's lifeboat, rigged with a well-patched, gaff-headed sail, an ancient outboard engine hanging off the stern and two oars lashed along the decks. I could see woolen underwear hanging on a rope beneath a kerosene lantern inside the cabin. Narrow shelves encircled the two sides and front end of the cabin and these shelves were filled with little starter-pots of green plants.

Somewhere he had been educated. He used a few French expressions in his conversation and had found space in his tiny, cluttered cabin for a shelf full of literary classics.

Of course, he was shunned by the more respectable, balding and somewhat paunchy owners of the luxurious, three-storey-high boats tied to the dock. Not one of their class, not of the boating fraternity, this derelict boat, this shabby, whiskered man. Somehow, I saw more to this man than what his appearance suggested, a past that held a story. But how do you ask a stranger to reveal himself, to open in conversation the closed chapters of his life?

I tried an easy opener, directed my conversation from his boat to mine.

I told him it was a replica of Joshua Slocum's famous *Spray*, the one he had sailed around the world.

"I recognized her as a *Spray*," he said. "My grandfather met old Slocum before he set off on his last voyage. He told me about him when I was a kid. In my first boat, a little ketch, I followed his track around the world. Been sailing on and off ever since."

"Do you always sail alone?" I asked.

"Oh yes, always single-handed. Met a lot of those old fellows out there sailing around by themselves: Dumas, Tabarly, Chichester, before he was famous. Met old Tilman once, down off Patagonia. He was a tough old bird."

My God! He was talking about my sailing heroes, men he had met when he had been younger, had sailed a boat not like his present relic, but one capable of long distances.

"Cost me a lot, all that sailing," he said. "No family, few friends, lonely days and nights. All I got left is this old lifeboat but I wouldn't trade my life for any other."

Then he looked seaward and said, "But this boat is all I need. The doc tells me I don't have much time left so I might as well go back to sea."

"In that little boat?" I asked with disbelief.

"It's big enough for as far as I am going," he said. Then, in a lowered voice, he added, "And I won't be coming back."

Just an old man in an old wooden boat, off on a voyage of no return, and I was the last man he would talk to.

Occasionally, I look at *Northern Spray* and think about a long, offshore voyage, knowing it would be capable of going anywhere. My wife understands these thoughts and has made this suggestion: "Don't go until you don't have to come back."

It's something to think about, to end on a dream.